MEMORIAL
DAYS

MEMORIAL DAYS

Geraldine Brooks

VIKING

VIKING
An imprint of Penguin Random House LLC
1745 Broadway, New York, NY 10019
penguinrandomhouse.com

Designed by Cassandra Garruzzo Mueller

LIBRARY OF CONGRESS CATALOGING-IN-PUBLICATION DATA

Names: Brooks, Geraldine, author.
Title: Memorial days : a memoir / Geraldine Brooks.
Description: [New York] : Viking, [2025]
Identifiers: LCCN 2024030251 (print) | LCCN 2024030252 (ebook) |
ISBN 9780593653982 (hardcover) | ISBN 9780593653999 (ebook)
Subjects: LCSH: Brooks, Geraldine. | Horwitz, Tony, 1958–2019—
Death and burial. | Women authors, Australian—Biography. |
Widows—Biography. | Grief in women.
Classification: LCC PR9619.3.B7153 Z46 2025 (print) |
LCC PR9619.3.B7153 (ebook) | DDC 823/.914 [B]—dc23/eng/20241028
LC record available at https://lccn.loc.gov/2024030251
LC ebook record available at https://lccn.loc.gov/2024030252

Printed in the United States of America
1st Printing

The authorized representative in the EU for product safety and compliance is
Penguin Random House Ireland, Morrison Chambers, 32 Nassau Street,
Dublin D02 YH68, Ireland, https://eu-contact.penguin.ie.

For Natty and Bizu

The only end some things have is the end you give them.

TIM WINTON, *THE RIDERS*

MEMORIAL
DAYS

May 27, 2019

WEST TISBURY

"Is this the home of Tony Horwitz?"

Yes

"Who am I speaking to?"

This is his wife

That is exact. The rest is a blur.

"Collapsed in the street . . . tried to resuscitate at the scene . . . brought to the hospital . . . couldn't revive him. . . ."

And, so, now he's in the OR. And, so, now we've admitted him for a procedure. And, so, now we're keeping him for observation.

So many things that logically should have followed.

But she says none of these things. Instead, the illogical thing:

He's dead.

No.

Not Tony. Not him. Not my husband out on the road energetically promoting his new book. My husband with the toned body of a six-day-a-week gym rat. The sixty-year-old who still wears clothes the same size as the day I met him in his twenties. My husband, younger than I am—hilarious, bursting with vitality. He's way too busy living. He cannot possibly be dead.

The resident's voice is flat, exhausted. She is impatient with me as I ask her to repeat what she has just said. It is, she tells me, the end of her shift. She gives me a number for the doctor who is coming on duty in this ER, five hundred miles away in Washington, D.C. She can't get me off the phone fast enough.

But Tony—I need to see him. Where will he be when I get there?

"We can't keep a body in the ER. It will be moved to the hospital morgue to be picked up by the DC medical examiner."

It. A body. She means Tony.

So how will I see him? I'm in Massachusetts, on an island. It's going to take me hours to get there—

She cuts me off.

"The DC police will need to talk to you. Make sure they can reach you."

And then she is gone.

At some moment in this call, I stood up from my desk. When the phone rang, at eighteen minutes past one, I'd only just sat down to work after a morning of distractions. I'd had a happy conversation on the phone with my older son, a recent college graduate, adventuring around the world and about to board a plane in Manila for the eight-hour flight to Sydney, where he would stay with my sister. A friend, Susanna, had come to borrow or return a book—I can't recall which. We'd gone down to the paddock to throw hay to the horses and hung around there, draped on the split rails, chatting.

I'd read a long email from Tony about the visit he'd made the day before to the Virginia village where we lived for ten years. It was mostly unpunctuated, gossipy, catching me up on the doings of our former neighbors—their tribulations with dry wells and divorces ("she refers to him as her was-band"). The email concluded:

"didn't wish self back there (if for no other reason, 90 degrees and 100 percent humidity, and still May) but heartened that it seems to have gently evolved while keeping history and quirk. tomorrow back to the grind and am now 2-3 episodes behind on Billions so you'll have rewatch upon return. love and hugs"

I'd hit send on my reply and finally opened the file titled Horse, the novel I was supposed to be writing.

Then, the phone.

Another distraction. I considered letting it go to voicemail.

But maybe there was a question my older son had forgotten to ask. My younger son was away at boarding school, sitting his end-of-year exams. Perhaps he needed something. I had to pick up.

The caller ID was hard to read in the bright sunlight. Only as I brought the handset close could I make out GW HSP on the display. Don't tell me I picked up a darn fundraising call. . . .

Now the dial tone burred. I stared at the handset. My legs started to shake. But I couldn't sit down. I paced across the room, feeling the howl forming in my chest. I needed to scream, weep, throw myself on the floor, rend my garments, tear my hair.

But I couldn't allow myself to do any of those things.

Because I had to do so many other things.

I stood there and suppressed that howl. Because I was alone, and no one could help me. And if I let go, if I fell, I might not be able to get back up.

In books and movies no one gets this news alone. Someone comes to the door. Someone makes sure you're sitting down, offers you water, asks whom you'd like them to call.

But no one had done me this kindness. A tired young doctor had picked up my husband's cell phone, on which he had never set up a passcode, and hit the speed dial for HOME.

The first brutality in what I would learn is a brutal, broken system.

Essendon

The small prop plane takes off from Melbourne's Essendon Airport. Suburban rooftops, container terminals, the industrialized mouth of the Yarra River. And then we pierce a flat layer of cloud and the view I'd hoped for, the glittering, island-studded Bass Strait, is obscured. All I can do is watch the mesmerizing blur of the propeller. A smear of concentric circles. The unlikely physics of flight.

I am headed to a shack on the farthest end of Flinders Island to do the unfinished work of grieving. I have come to realize that what I did that day in late May 2019 and what I was obliged to do in the days and months that followed has exacted an invisible price. I am going to this remote island to pay it.

In the confines of the small plane I overhear snatches of conversation from my fellow travelers:

"I've got a hundred acres, it's quite a big bit of dirt."

"No one's prolly fished that spot since we were there last year."

"You can have the views, or you can have the bars, but you gotta consider the cell tower if you're building a place."

"All the pines are gone."

"What d'ya mean, gone?"

"I mean gone, mate. Not there."

Tony died on Memorial Day, the American holiday that falls on the last Monday in May and honors the war dead.

When I get to Flinders Island, I will begin my own memorial days. I am taking something that our culture has stopped freely giving: the right to grieve. To shut out the world and its demands. To remember my love and to feel the immensity of his loss. "Grief is praise," writes Martín Prechtel in his book *The Smell of Rain on Dust*, "because it is the natural way love honors what it misses."

I haven't honored Tony enough, because I have not permitted myself the time and space for a grief deep enough to reflect our love.

This will be, finally, the time when I will not have to prepare a face for the faces that I meet. The place where I will not have to pretend that things are normal and that I am okay. Because it has been more than three years and, contrary to appearances, I am not at all okay. I have come to realize that my life since Tony's death has been one endless, exhausting performance. I have cast myself in a role: *woman being normal*. I've moved around in public acting out a series of convincing scenes: PTO mum, conservation commissioner, author on tour. But nothing has been normal. Here, finally, the long-running show goes on hiatus.

I have been trapped in the *maytzar*, the narrow place of the Hebrew scriptures. In the Psalms, the singer cries out to God from the narrow place and is answered from the "wideness" of God. Our English word "anguish" means the same thing as the Hebrew *maytzar*. It is from the Latin for narrowness, strait, restriction. I have not allowed myself the wild wideness of an elaborate, florid, demonstrative grief. Instead, it has been this long feeling of constriction, of holding it in and tamping it down and not letting it show.

I am not a deist. No god will answer my cries. The wideness I seek is in nature, in quiet, in time.

And I have chosen this place, this island, deliberately. Before I met Tony, my life had begun directing me here. Falling in love with him derailed that life, set me on an entirely different course. Now I might glimpse what I have been missing, walk that untraveled road, consider the person I might have become.

Alone on this island at the ends of the earth, maybe, I will finally be able to break out of the *maytzar*. But first I will need to get back to that moment in my sunlit study when I refused to allow myself to howl.

That howl has become the beast in the basement of my heart. I need to find a way to set it free.

May 27, 2019

WEST TISBURY

"The DC police will need to talk to you. Make sure they can reach you."

But she hadn't asked for, and I hadn't given her, my cell phone, so that meant I had to stay by the landline and wait for that call. In between, I searched for my mobile—in those days I barely ever used it—and began to do what needed to be done.

My first call was to the airport. It's a small rural airport, and I know the people who work the desks by name. Could they get me off the island? Was there any chance, any seat at all?

Not on Memorial Day weekend. That long weekend is the unofficial beginning of summer. Every flight off Martha's Vineyard that afternoon had been booked for months.

I would have to take the ferry to the mainland and a car to Boston—three hours—and hope I could get on a flight from there to DC. The next ferry was at two thirty p.m. I could make it if I dumped the car in an illegal parking spot.

Then the home phone rang. Detective Evelyn from the DC police. He was gentle, considerate. I was thankful for this unexpected kindness after the brusque doctor. He was able to tell me exactly where Tony had been walking when he collapsed, and that the first to see him lying on the ground was a former Vietnam medic who yelled for someone to call 911 as he checked for vital signs. The detective described how women from the yoga studio across the road ran out with a defibrillator and in minutes two ambulances arrived—one from DC and one from Chevy Chase, because Tony had collapsed right on the line between the District of Columbia and the Maryland suburbs. Both teams of EMTs had worked on him—the detective was not sure for how long—before they rushed him to the downtown emergency room.

He asked me some questions about Tony's health, about why he was in DC. He explained that because there were no witnesses to his collapse, there would need to be an autopsy to rule out foul play. I asked if I could speak with the man who found Tony. He said he would try to put me in touch. I told him I was leaving for the ferry and gave him my cell phone number.

Then I looked for the number for Tony's brother, Josh. He and the rest of the Horwitz clan had gone to Maine for his daughter's college graduation. Small mercies: Ellie, Tony's mum, was with them.

She would be surrounded by loving support when she heard this unspeakable news.

Tony had been staying in Josh's empty house in Chevy Chase. The Memorial Day holiday weekend had given him a welcome break in the relentless schedule he had been following since his book's publication. He'd done eight events in seven days, crossing the entire country. All his emails mentioned how exhausted he was after getting up early for flights, staying late at book signings, then heading out for drinks with the old friends who inevitably turned up at those events.

When he finally reached his brother's house, he slept for hours and called me to say how good it felt to have had some rest. By Sunday afternoon, feeling revived, he'd gone to visit our onetime neighbors in Waterford, the tiny village of eighty or so families in the foothills of the Blue Ridge, where we'd lived for a decade. That leisurely Memorial Day Monday, all he had to do was show up for a dinner in his honor with Washington friends. The next day he would be back on tour. He had a slew of interviews lined up starting early in the morning, then a book event that evening at the famed DC bookstore, Politics and Prose.

But there was no next day.

"Northampton Street?" Josh, stunned, whispered, when I told him where Tony had collapsed. "That's just a block from my house."

Josh, Tony's older brother, had matured from an unruly youth into the mensch of the family, the man you needed in a crisis. He said he would find a flight from Maine, leave right away. His sister, Erica, and her husband, David, would bring Ellie to DC by car. His wife, Ericka, would take their daughters to their various planes: the two young women had their jobs and school to get back to. He said he would likely reach his house before I would. He sensed the panic in my voice. "Take a minute, think what you should pack. You might be there awhile."

Despite his advice I left the house in what I was wearing, and would be wearing, for the next three days. Some underwear, a toothbrush—I couldn't think further than that. I had to make the two thirty ferry to get the last seat on the flight I had booked to DC. I called my neighbors, Fred and Jeanne, told them what had happened, and asked if they would look after our dogs and the horses. They will, of course they will. They will come right over.

On the boat I called the number for the resident that the first doctor had given me, the doctor who had relieved her for the evening shift. This young man had no idea who I was or what I was talking about. He was clearly up to his eyeballs in other people's emergencies.

When I asked if Tony's body would still be at the hospital when I got there, he snapped at me: "How should I know?"

I don't know why I expected better than this, but I did.

First, do no harm.

FLINDERS ISLAND

As I step off the plane, a gust of wind wants my hat. I clutch it just in time. This island—this gorgeous, haunted island—sits square in the path of the Roaring Forties, winds hauled down from the equator toward the South Pole, blowing westerly along this latitude, unobstructed by any landmass. It's February, late summer, and the noontime sun is warm on my face. But it's windy enough to blow the milk out of your tea.

I have been here only once before, with Tony, when I was researching a novel that touched on the island's tragic history—a novel that I never wrote.

We were both struck by the beauty of this island; we both loved the place. But like everything to do with Australia, I loved it more than he did. Tony was American to his core, and while I managed to get him to live in Sydney for extended periods a few times during our marriage, I couldn't make him into an Australian. As much as I expected, then hoped, then longed for him to see things differently, he never came to appreciate the country as I do. In his journal in 1994, ten years into our marriage, he wrote: "A stunningly civilized land next to America but at the same time smug and sun-struck . . . not a place I want to live, something I can't even discuss with G. without her becoming tearful or angry."

It was one of the few things we argued about, and it was an argument I lost. Marriage is constant compromise. On many important matters Tony was the one who gave way. For years he shaped his career around mine, following me first to Cleveland, then to Sydney, then to Cairo. But on this most fundamental issue, he prevailed. I never fully reconciled to it.

"We imprint like baby goslings, on a type of horizon. On a type of sky," Barbara Kingsolver told a reporter who asked her what she loved about Appalachia. My imprinted horizon is the Pacific Ocean, framed by sandstone headlands and sinuous gum trees; my pellucid sky contains the Southern Cross. But it's more than landscape for me. It's also a national personality. An informal, self-deprecating style of moving through the world with a grin on your face and a hand ready to be chucked back to help the mate who might be lagging. A national consensus that tends to value the good of the many over the desires of the individual.

We each loved our own country, but he relied on his. It was his muse. It fed the work that was his passion. That work was relating the American past to its present, something he did with extraordinary prescience, insight, and wit. My work is mostly in my own head and can be done anywhere. So, I accepted an expatriation I did not want and raised my sons in a country whose values and choices often felt incomprehensible. If I'd never met Tony, never loved him with passionate commitment, I think there is a very good chance that I would have ended up on Flinders Island, instead of Martha's Vineyard, where we'd finally put down our roots after years of vagabonding around the world as foreign correspondents. Most places we chose to live had this in common: the profligate sparkle of water encountered unexpectedly when you turn a corner, crest a hill. The first homes of our married life were on the Balmain peninsula in Sydney; in Egypt, we lived on an island in the Nile; and Martha's Vineyard, eight miles off the coast of Massachusetts, was the island where we finally settled and raised our kids. More than half our married life was spent there.

One reason I have chosen to come to Flinders for these memorial days, and not some other isolated place, is to interrogate the cost of my compromise. If this lovely island was, in fact, the destination of my road not taken, what would that life have looked like, as I raised Australian kids and wrote Australian books? What would have been gained, and what would have been lost? It's not really possible to answer these questions, but they nag me. Returning here is the necessary, if not the sufficient, condition for thinking about this more clearly than my gauzy old memories of the place allow.

Inside Flinders Island's tiny airport terminal, I sign for a rental car that, I'm warned by the young woman at the desk, "has some damage." On the paperwork the diagram of the vehicle has black pen marks indicating dings on almost every panel. It's easy to find; it's the one with the front bumper that's been ripped in half and stitched back together with the auto equivalent of Steri-Strips. Such are the make-dos of a remote rural place where almost every material thing you need arrives on a barge on a Wednesday. I admire this: it's very Australian. Suddenly I have an earworm: John Williamson's anthem, "True Blue":

> Will you tie it up with wire,
> just to keep the show on the road?

The first stop I make is to pick up food. The shack I am renting is almost thirty miles from the nearest store, and half of that is tricky dirt road, undrivable above about ten miles an hour from dusk to dawn if you don't want to slaughter the nocturnal wildlife—the wallabies, pademelons, and wombats who thrive here.

The woman who hands me the provisions also works for the owner of the shack—that's how things go among the small population here—so I get directions: "Turn right back up by the airport and just keep going." It's unlocked. "We don't lock anything." My kind of place. When we bought our 1740s home on the Vineyard, the doors had never had locks installed.

As I drive north along the west coast of the island, I notice what is like and what is unlike the Vineyard. Both islands are rimmed with beaches—some broad and sandy, some intimate and covelike. The Vineyard's year-round population is much larger—maybe fifteen times greater than that of Flinders Island—and the summer influx of tourists and second-home owners swells it enormously. Still, both islands have wide tracts of farmland rolling toward ocean and acres of unspoiled woods and marshes. The houses are similar in some ways; modest beach cottages and farmsteads, though in recent years many of the Vineyard's unpretentious homes have been demolished in favor of lavish summer compounds out of scale with island tradition.

The most striking difference is the geology. The Vineyard is a terminal moraine—low hills of clay soils and boulders pushed out into the ocean by an ancient glacier. Flinders is part of an island chain that is the remnant of a drowned land bridge that once connected Tasmania to the Australian mainland. It has a rocky mountain spine slung between two soaring peaks—one north, one south—thrusting into the sky at either end of the island like exclamations.

As the northern peak, Mount Killiecrankie, looms into view, I know I am nearing my destination. I turn off the main road and bump down the steep track to the shack.

I am all alone here in this beautiful place. Where Tony should be, hauling the wheelie bag, already restless and impatient for the first adventure. I have a sudden sharp memory of him, from the last time we visited Tasmania. He'd decided to use the vacation to break his addiction to nicotine gum, and when we couldn't immediately find the right room at the hotel we'd booked, he'd stamped his foot and sat down on his wheelie bag, grumpy and petulant as a toddler. The boys and I had laughed at him and told him to go get some Nicorette.

I smile at that recollection. Toward the end of that vacation, we'd sent the boys back to Sydney and celebrated our thirtieth wedding anniversary alone together on a wild beach on Tassie's east coast.

Now I wrestle the wheelie bag over the rough ground by myself. I let sadness come and accept it. This is how it is now. Lonely.

But right on its heels, yapping like an ill-disciplined terrier, a quer-ulous inner voice: *What's up with you? You're lucky to be here, to have the means and the time to do this. And look at that view!*

The shack is just three simple rooms, built of mismatched timber. It sits at the southern end of a deep, goblet-shaped bay, looking di-rectly across at Mount Killiecrankie, a muscular swell of granite surging out of the sea. The boulders are striated with vivid *Calo-placa*, an algae-fungi symbiosis that stains the rock in bright bands of tangerine. I stand and stare, gobsmacked by the beauty of the orange rock and various blues of the water, as shifting and lumi-nous as the colors in peacocks' plumage.

I put the food in the small fridge and set out to walk the beach. This turns out to be more of a hike than it looks. The deep curve conceals its true length. When I leave the shack, it's two p.m. It's four thirty when I get back. At low tide the fine white sand is firm underfoot, the beach wide and expansive. There is only one other person. In the distance, a woman plays with her dog, throwing a ball. I get close enough to see that the dog is ginger and white, like a Brittany spaniel. The beach is so wide it seems impolite to change my trajectory. I do not encroach on them as I pass. When I turn to look, they've vanished up some unseen track in the dunes, and I am all alone. I feel how extraordinary that is. Most beaches as beautiful as this have been developed, so these miles of high dunes are a bit of a marvel—a globally rare example of pristine coastal health. My shack is one of just a handful of simple structures confined to a small area of the rocky southern end of the beach.

The dunes eventually give way to upthrusting granite, the sand replaced by rock shelves and pools. Cuttlefish skeletons have been blown into crevices. Some are a foot long, abraded by the wind to resemble the contours of topographical models. A shiny curve like a draftsman's spline catches my eye. It is the edge of a perfect abalone shell. When I lift it out of the sand it glows in ripples, iridescent pinks and greens.

All this, I want to share with Tony. I want him alive beside me, to feel the sting as the wind picks up, to bundle up on the deck and hold my hand through the late twilight, to watch the moon rise, lustrous as a pearl, over Mount Killiecrankie.

I have many friends with good marriages. Long ones like ours. Lucky people, like we were. They have raised their kids, done good work—usually in the arts or the media—and, in their sixties, have money and the time to enjoy each other. I'm happy for them when they post their lovely pictures, sipping coffee in a square in Sienna, exploring Kakadu, scrambling over a lava field in Hawaii, canoeing the Okavango. I am also envious.

Tony and I had a bit less than two years as empty nesters, after our younger son implored us to let him go to the boarding school that had recruited him for lacrosse. I was sorry he chose to go. I came late to mothering and loved it; I did not want to be cheated of four more years on the daily job. I was also skeptical of elite private schools and their superprivileged progeny. But Bizu had a talent, and a dream. It seemed churlish to stand in his way.

It turned out to be a blissful time for the two of us, with no one to consider but ourselves. For the first time in decades, we could go out, spontaneously, to dinner or a movie, instead of riding shotgun on homework and bedtime. We made a wonderful trip to Oxford, where Tony was giving a speech on historical memory and the arguments over Civil War monuments. We walked cobbled laneways of golden stone, got into lively discussions in the low-ceilinged pubs, and plotted how we might get back there for a longer stay.

What big plans we had. How many more adventures there would be for us, just as soon as Tony's book was finished.

Plans. Oh, those.

COVID taught all of us the futility of plans. I've become superstitious about the word in case I hex myself. The old saying—*If you want to make God laugh, make plans*—has never seemed so true. And yet, by now, we would have been making them. Together.

Instead, I am here. Missing him. Alone.

May 27, 2019

VINEYARD HAVEN FERRY

Try to think. Try to think. Out of the blur of overwhelming emotion, I struggled to work out what I needed to do.

There was Sally in Georgetown, who believed she would be hosting a dinner for Tony and ten of our friends in fewer than five hours. There was Sarah at Penguin Press, who had created the intricate web of his book tour, its intersecting strands of interviews, appearances, plane reservations, all now undone. And Kris, our literary agent, our old friend. She would know what else needed to be done on the professional front. Oh, and the Vineyard friends whose celebration I was supposed to be heading to, even as the boat horn sounded and we pulled away from the slip.

In the winter I would have known a lot of people on this boat. There would have been conversations, catch-ups, pleasantries during the forty-five-minute journey across Vineyard Sound to Woods

Hole on Cape Cod. But at the end of the Memorial Day weekend, the boat was packed with tourists. I was able to find a seat amid strangers, where I did not have to have conversations I was incapable of having.

It is a beautiful crossing, the deep notch of the harbor giving way to a wide strait of roiling currents. Gulls dive and hover over the steamship as it navigates between colorful buoys that mark safe passage through rocky shoals. In the years we'd come to the Vineyard as summer visitors, Tony and I had loved this crossing, looked forward to it. Going to the island, the boat trip marked the beginning of vacation in a tangible way, putting a stretch of ocean between stress and relaxation. Standing out on the foredeck, hugging each other, hair tousled in the salt wind, we'd breathe deep and let go of work anxiety, the tensions of the real world. On the journey back it was a period of contentment, a moment for savoring the experiences we'd had together, the pleasant coda to good times.

But on that day all I wanted was for the crossing to be over. As we neared the mainland I punched details into my ride app, and as soon as we docked, I sprinted down the gangway to the waiting car. I barely had my seat belt fastened when my friend Susanna called me. The Vineyard is a small place. Its grapevine had done its work. Someone at the airport had mentioned something to someone. Now Tony's death had been reported in the online edition of the local paper.

This was terrible. I had not reached our sons yet. Nathaniel, the one on the plane to Sydney, would be spared this news for a few more hours. How desperately I wanted to spare both of them. Bizu was only sixteen, a high school sophomore. He would be done with school in just two and a half days. He is our adopted son and when he came home to us, at five, he had already survived a lifetime's full measure of loss. I explained to Susanna my mad impulse to withhold this news, to let him finish his school year, to keep it from him until I could get to him, hold him. No, she said firmly. "You have to tell him. Right now. They live on their phones, you know that. Do you want him to see it online?"

I called the principal of his school, Peter, a caring man. He said he would bring Bizu to his office and surround him with support. Then they would call me back so that I could break the news. For the next few minutes I cowered in the back seat of a stranger's car and imagined my son's torment. What would he think when pulled out of class by his advisor and taken to the principal's office? I pictured him, walking anxiously across the manicured grounds of that lovely school, past flower beds flossed with spring bloom. His last few minutes before his world collapsed. His birth father, a soldier in the army of Ethiopia, had died when he was an infant. Tony was the only father Bizu had ever known. When we brought him home—undernourished, tiny—Tony had carried him on his shoulders everywhere for almost a year. What words could I possibly use to tell him?

That call, the sound of my son's sobs, in a place too far to reach for him and hug him, was a new depth of darkness on a dark, dark day.

At the airport I walked in a daze through the rigmarole of check-in, TSA screening, down the long familiar corridor of Logan Terminal C, where I know every Cibo, every Wolfgang Puck, every Hudson. Holiday travelers swarmed the gate lounge, not a seat vacant. As I waited to board, Detective Evelyn called me back. Mr. Ryan, the former medic who had been the first to reach Tony, had agreed to speak to me. He was waiting for my call. I found the quietest, most private place I could, a corner wedged behind a pillar, and turned my face to the wall as I entered the number.

"When I caught sight of him, he was lying prone on the sidewalk, and at first I thought he was looking for something under his car. Then I saw his glasses. They were a foot and a half away from him. I knew something must be wrong."

Mr. Ryan recounted how he had rushed over and taken Tony's pulse—faint and intermittent—and noted labored, convulsive breaths. He called out to a woman at the nearby yoga studio to dial 911. There was no sign of any trauma—the fall must have been gentle, maybe Tony had dropped to his knees and then crumpled slowly forward. His arms were at his sides, indicating he hadn't attempted to break his fall, or even been aware of falling. Linda, the yoga instructor, rushed out with the studio's defibrillator, and they started CPR. Then—"I think it was less than five minutes"—the paramedics arrived and took over.

There, or at the ER, an endotracheal tube was inserted. There, or at the ER, multiple ECG pads were applied, multiple IV lines inserted. Someone had administered amiodarone, the drug of last resort for ventricular fibrillation.

"They worked hard and well at the scene for a good half hour. But he wasn't conscious and there was no pulse." He paused. "The women from the yoga place were stroking his head. They were very affectionate. Careful and caring."

I was too choked up to respond to this, so I garbled some thanks to him for trying to help Tony, and for taking my call.

"I had a sister," he said. "She died alone in her apartment. It's been terrible, not knowing what her last moments were like. I'm glad I can tell you this."

FLINDERS ISLAND

I can't sleep, despite the absolute quiet of this place. I have intentionally put myself back where I was on the worst day of my life. It is what I came here to do; to uncover every memory of that time and experience the full measure of the grief I had denied myself.

I get up around two a.m. and walk out under the almost full moon. The garden is occupied by a mob of grazing wallabies. They bound off, chased by their own moon shadows, and I am guilty that I have disturbed them. I go back to bed, thinking to read for a while. I have brought some books with me. Books gifted by well-meaning people that recount the grim aftermath of losing a spouse: *The Light of the World* by Elizabeth Alexander, *A Widow's Story* by Joyce Carol Oates. We already had a copy of Joan Didion's memoir, *The Year of Magical Thinking*. It's a tattered galley—the cheaply bound, uncorrected proofs of forthcoming books that publishers send out to critics before the hardcover is published. Tony was a judge for the nonfiction category of the National Book Award that year. This book of Didion's won.

No thanks to judge Tony, apparently. On the first page of the galley, Tony has scrawled:

Name & product dropping. Padded.

I'd been reluctant to pick the book up, but now Tony's brusque dismissal of this acclaimed memoir makes me smile. Throughout the galley he has underlined all the mentions of celebrities and luxury goods and marked up the passages of prose he considered overwrought. There's a lot of marking.

But as I read it, I can't agree with his dismissive evaluation. Didion's experience so closely chimes with my own. The long marriage, the intertwined careers, the sudden disorienting loss. Give her a break, I want to say to him. She worked in the movies; her friends happened to be famous. She can't help that.

The bed lamp isn't strong, so I can't read for very long. But I know I will return to this book, and I'm glad for Tony's disparaging scrawls. I feel as if we are reading it together, having a friendly disagreement.

It was a rare point of difference between us, this marking of books. I am careful with mine. I seek out first printings, autographed copies. I take the dust jackets off new hardbacks while I read them, to keep them in pristine condition. I would no sooner write in a book than deliberately gouge a scratch in an antique table or scribble on a painting. Tony was the opposite. He read with pen in hand, scrawling his thoughts all over the place. I am glad of this now. If I pick up one of his books that I haven't yet read, I can know what he thought of it.

When I finally fall asleep, I don't wake till late. It's a gray, windy morning, and the sea is high. I have only a loose notion of how I will spend my time here. I will walk and reflect, taking whatever solace nature cares to offer me. I will write down everything I can recall about Tony's death and its aftermath. I will allow myself time and space to think about our marriage and to experience the emotions I've suppressed.

As I wait for the ebb tide, I eat granola, which is not something I ever eat at home. I'm not sure why I included it in my grocery order since it is as chewy and tasteless as I remember. I set off in the opposite direction of the walk I took yesterday, going west around the rock shelf, looking at the teeming life in the tidal pools.

The limpets are huge and designer-striped in shades of sienna, cream, and russet. There are gleaming sheets of mica and a smooth, yellow intrusion of stone with a cube-shaped crystal that I later learn is orthoclase, potassium feldspar. There are pockets of samphire— sea asparagus—the ocean's best crunchy, salty snack. I get around the headland and a new vista discloses itself, a high wooded bluff with eucalyptus and casuarinas, pierced by a dagger-shaped inlet. It is challenging, rock-hopping the granite boulders. When I get to a deep chasm, though it isn't that wide, I have second thoughts about jumping it. If I slip, well, it's remote out here. No one would be coming to haul me out. Instead, I head inland, inhaling the scent of the bush, once again disturbing wallabies.

But then I reach a pile of slash. Trees have been cleared here, many trees. A new road has gone in. I follow it up the bluff. It's a steep walk. Although there are occasional fine views from rocky outcrops, I feel dispirited by all the dead trees, all the destruction. Roads are fragmenters of habitat, pathways for invasive species, eroders of soil, silters of watercourses. The bush here looks pristine. I see no invasive species. How soon, I wonder, will this new road change that? And then I see where the road is apparently headed, and my heart sinks. Way across the valley is something still rare on this island—a gargantuan multi-building compound. All alone on the otherwise unspoiled mountainside. This is the access road. It's obscene that one big house should be allowed to cause so much damage. Martha's Vineyard was like Flinders not so long ago. But so many new mansions just like that one have put native flora and fauna under pressure from introduced species. Ponds are eutrophying from the pressure of too many humans.

When I reach the highest point, before the road dips to cross the valley, I head back down the hill. I won't go that way again.

Et in Arcadia ego.

May 27, 2019

Tony was born in George Washington University Medical Center on June 9, 1958. He was pronounced dead there at 12:38 p.m. on May 27, 2019. His father, Norman Horwitz, practiced and taught neurosurgery at that hospital. His grandfather Alec was a general surgeon there.

Tony, who traveled the world as a foreign correspondent, covering stories from sniper pits in Sarajevo and boats under shelling in Beirut harbor, who ducked rifle fire during the Romanian revolution and reported on two wars in the Persian Gulf, who hitchhiked across the Australian outback and followed the Pacific voyages of Captain James Cook from the Arctic Circle to the edge of the Antarctic ice shelf, had come home to die. He had been pronounced dead in the hospital where he was born, after collapsing a scant few blocks from the brown-shingled Victorian house in Chevy Chase in which he grew up.

He died on a Monday. Statistically, that is the most common day to die of cardiac arrest. Men, particularly, are 20 percent more likely to have a heart attack on that day. No one knows exactly why.

I went to the hospital reception desk and asked to see my husband's body. I was directed to a door just off the ER waiting room, which was teeming with misery on this public holiday. I passed through snatches of dire dialogue between patients and triage nurses. In a closet-sized office a harried staffer squinted at me. "You're the third one asking." I learned that dear friends in the city—Bob and Elsa, Joel and Mary—had rushed here, separately, hoping to sit vigil with Tony. "I'm afraid I have to tell you what I told them: no one is allowed." He spread his hands. "It's DC, we get gunshot casualties, angry people . . ." He trailed off as he saw my face crumple. "Your husband mightn't even be here now. Medical examiner might've already picked up. Best to call them in the morning."

He handed me a plastic bag. I stared at it, baffled.

"His effects."

A pair of flip-flops, a page of crumpled newspaper, his phone, his glasses, his wallet.

I reached blindly for the chair behind me and collapsed into it.

"I'm sorry," I sputtered. "But I've just been struggling to get here ever since . . . and now . . . and now you say I can't see him. . . ." The man raised a hand. "Take all the time you want." He went out for a while and came back with a paper cup of water. For the second time that day, I tried to pull myself together. I was taking up space in this man's office; I needed to leave. I swiped at my eyes and once again stifled the howl my body craved.

I stepped out into the humid dusk of the DC evening and walked around the hospital to the loading dock. I did not believe that the city coroner had picked up Tony. Not on a public holiday. I had a mad impulse to sneak in there, steal some scrubs, find the morgue.

Be with him.

It is the kind of thing Tony would do. As a reporter in the first Gulf War, he bribed a dry cleaner to sell him a Saudi army uniform (only Saudis send their fatigues to dry cleaners, only Tony noticed this and acted on it). Dressed as a soldier, he got to the front lines and was the only American reporter with the first wave of Kuwaiti troops as they liberated their city.

I stood there for a long time, trying to muster the courage to do this mad thing. Traffic streamed behind me; ambulances arrived and departed in a noisy urgency of swirling lights and bleating sirens.

I'm not Tony. I couldn't channel his chutzpah. I turned and hailed a cab for Josh's house.

FLINDERS ISLAND

In the middle of the night, my American cell phone rings. How is that even possible? I have it on airplane mode. People aren't supposed to be able to call me here. (My kids have my Australian number for emergencies: only a handful of people know it.) I grope in the dark to answer.

It's my friend Jim, a comedy writer, calling from Los Angeles, asking if I would read the draft of a rom-com he's written and give him notes. He has no idea I'm on an island in the Bass Strait, trying to mourn my husband who has been dead for more than three years.

It's way too complicated to explain, and anyway, I don't want to make him feel bad. So, I say the easy thing: Sure, send it.

I hang up, thinking how amused Tony would be by this massive disconnect. I imagine his glee; how he would take this story and massage it into a bit, to regale a dinner party and delight our friends.

Of all the things I miss about Tony—his lilting speaking voice, his gentle hands—it's this most of all: He made me laugh every single day. He could see absurdity, puncture pomposity, pull off practical jokes of maddening plausibility. Our family learned to beware the date April 1 and to defend against scams so elaborate they might involve a newspaper article, mocked up in perfect typeface, scooping me on a news story I'd been toiling over, or a convincingly dramatized phone call from a contractor saying that the new renovation work in the kitchen wasn't built to code and would have to be demolished. Kids in our neighborhood loved to visit on Halloween for the elaborate scares Tony would create: one year, he made gruesome dummy corpses for the front garden and then dressed up in similar ketchup-smeared rags to lie on the lawn himself. As the kids came down the path, his "dummy" would spring to life, hollering.

While writing, he could be intense: a perfectionist, woe betide anyone who disturbed him. The best you'd get was a cranky grunt. He worked in a bright book-lined space we'd carved out in what was once a cow barn. I wrote in a study upstairs in our old house. I'd hear him clatter into the kitchen several times a day, quickly grabbing coffee to fuel his effort. I did not try to interact with him during these missions: I knew from experience it would be an unrewarding encounter; the only time this hypersocial being was antisocial.

I would generally write during school hours—a practice I continued even after the boys no longer needed my afternoon hovering.

The routine suited me. I'd stop work by about four and start planning dinner. Sometime after five I'd look up through the kitchen
window and see Tony walking down the worn path from the barn,
closed laptop tucked under his arm. I'd know that the fun was
about to begin. I'd open the wine and we'd pick up the conversation wherever we'd left it. Every night had a party feel: exuber-
ant, funny.

I miss those laughs at the end of the day.

Sometimes Bizu cracks me up in exactly the way Tony did—he
also has an eye for the absurd and savage comic timing. But like a
hungry person on a diet, I crave more. Friends who make me laugh,
like Jim in LA, have become essential to me.

Jim's early-morning call is a reminder of how hard it is to shut the
world out. Before I left home, I tried to tie up every loose end, pay
every bill, answer every email. But when I logged on one last time
to put up an AWAY message, I was deluged with new busywork.
What flights do I want for a literary festival in May? The payment
for an essay I wrote in December didn't go through because they
need me to use a new portal for my invoice. A tradie I thought I'd
paid has re-sent his bill and I had to go back and check my
records.

The same old morass: *Getting and spending, we lay waste our powers.*

I deal with what can be done quickly, then put up the AWAY message. This time, they will all have to wait.

I have no idea how that one phone call got through from Los Angeles. When I found this shack, the online listing warned that cell service on this end of the island was very poor, the wi-fi spotty. As far as I was concerned that made the place precisely fit for purpose. But by the time I got here some months later, the national telecom had completed a major upgrade.

The whole island now has decent coverage.

A violent night. Lashing rain, winds loud as a train. The little wooden shack—banged together with recycled doors, salvaged timbers, and repurposed metalwork—groans with the power of the storm.

Rain is precious here. It is the sole supplier of drinking water, and as I imagine this deluge sluicing down the tin roof and filling the tank with that essential commodity, I fall back to sleep.

This morning, I start to do the work that I have come here to do. I open my laptop and drag the cursor back through my sent emails to the dreadful date, May 27, 2019. All the normal stuff, and then the email I sent to Sally in Georgetown.

> Header: *Terrible news.*

> *Tony died. The hospital just called. Apparently a massive heart attack. I will be in touch when I know more.*

I keep reading. How quickly the ripples of loss widened. How swift the first brokenhearted reactions of friends. From Frankie:

There's so much I want to say to you, but for now, just this: I will always think of Tony as I saw him last, golden and electric, backlit by the sunset at Lambert's Cove.

I read this and I want to stop. But I make myself keep going, accepting the tightness in my chest, the radiating pain from my gut.

And as I read on, I see how quickly I fell into what would become my rote response to condolences.

We were so lucky.

There it was. My defensive shield already deployed, and Tony not three hours dead.

I have vaulted right over denial, anger, bargaining, and depression and landed in the soft sands of acceptance.

I now know that even as I wrote those words, I was in denial. I didn't believe he was dead. I expected him to come bursting through the door, throwing clothes out of his bag, loudly regaling me with funny tales from the road.

That vault I had attempted was impossible. Those sands were quicksand.

CHEVY CHASE

At Josh's house Tony's bag lay open in the hallway, just as he'd left it. He had found time to buy two new linen shirts. Nice ones. The tags were still on them, these lovely shirts he would never wear.

Everyone was in the kitchen: Josh; his sister, Erica; her husband, David; and Ellie, the matriarch, drawn and diminished. When we hugged, she felt frail. I told her she raised a wonderful man. It was a peculiar thing to say. I must have thought so even as I was saying it, because I don't remember anything else that was said that night.

We were all staggering. It was late. After a little while Erica and David took Ellie home to her nearby apartment, where they would stay with her. Josh's wife, Ericka, had offered to pick up Bizu from his boarding school in the morning, after she dropped her daughters at the airport on the way back from Maine. Friends who lived near his school had volunteered to go get him, keep him with them for the night. But he said no. He had chosen to wait alone in his dorm.

Josh and I slumped on the sofa. He'd lost his brother. I'd lost the love of my life. We'd both lost a best friend.

Tony and Josh were as tight as I imagine it is possible for brothers to be. Josh and I are the same age, three years older than Tony. The baby brother, the bridegroom I cradle-snatched when he was only twenty-six. It wasn't supposed to go this way.

Who will die first? It is the refrain in the Don DeLillo novel *White Noise*, constantly asked by the married protagonists, Jack and Babette. Because I was older, because I survived cancer in my forties, I did not ask that question. I just assumed it would be me.

I got Tony's wallet from the hospital's plastic bag. In it was a receipt from Bread and Chocolate, a bakery and coffee shop just a twelve-minute walk from Josh's house. The time stamp was blurred but it looked like 11:16 a.m. When Tony asked for that bill, only one hour and twenty-two minutes would pass before he would be pronounced dead on a hospital gurney.

That last email I received from him had been sent around ten thirty the night before. It was the funny, gossipy one about his adventures that day in Waterford. In the morning, when I read it, he was already on his way to the coffee shop. He never saw my reply. He'd probably slept in, then ventured out for a leisurely brunch. The receipt tells us he had a Classic Shakshuka, a large OJ, a coffee. His last meal on this earth. He paid that bill, left the café, walked for two minutes back toward his brother's house, and collapsed. The crumpled piece of newspaper in the plastic bag must have been in his hand when he fell. It was a long article, making the case for reparations for enslavement.

Josh had spoken with Tony that morning, probably minutes before he'd left the house. Josh had just encountered a group of Civil War reenactors, the subject of Tony's earlier book *Confederates in the Attic*. An unlikely sight on the streets of Lewiston, Maine. He'd called Tony, and they'd laughed about it.

Before Josh got my call, he had planned to stay behind and help his daughter clean out her dorm. Instead, he'd given a driver a hundred bucks to get him to the Portland airport in time for the last flight to DC. He did not tell me that night, but months later he said he was frantic to get to the house before I did in case there was anything to upset me about the way Tony had left it.

As we slumped on his couch, Josh and I were wakeful, weepy, exhausted but afraid to attempt to sleep. Finally, in the small hours, I went upstairs to lie in the bed Tony slept in the night before. It was unmade, just as he had left it. I buried my face in the pillow, imagining the weight of his head, the length of his body. I didn't sleep. Josh's wife had collected Madame Alexander dolls as a kid. Arrayed on the dresser they stared at me, wide-eyed, forever sleepless.

I fretted for Bizu, alone in his tiny dorm room. I hoped he wasn't regretting his choice to stay at school. It was hard to think about him holding on to this enormity until his aunt could get there the next morning.

And Nathaniel, who would soon be landing in Sydney. I hadn't been able to reach my sister there; I'd left messages for her to call me. Australia was going to be Nathaniel's last stop on the six-month, postcollege adventure he was having with his girlfriend before he started work mid-June as a biotech entrepreneur in Boston. He was going to get home in just a couple more weeks, in time for Tony's sixty-first birthday on June 9. It was the longest that father and son had gone without seeing each other. Now they would never see each other again.

But I would not be the one to break this news to Nathaniel. When he landed in Sydney and turned on his phone, the first message he saw, after two missed calls from me, was a text from a Vineyard friend:

Really loved your pops.

My sister, rushing to an early-morning tennis game, had not checked her messages when she woke up, so had not seen mine. Nathaniel and his girlfriend showed up on her doorstep sobbing.

Just before dawn my phone lit up with a message from her. Was I awake, could she call? I said best not to, in case Josh, in the bedroom nearby, had managed to fall into a fragile slumber.

She wanted to jump on a plane with Nathaniel and be beside me. I asked her to wait.

I suspect this gets harder, I wrote. *I'll need you more then.*

FLINDERS ISLAND

As I started to make dinner, I realized I hadn't planned as well as I thought and was missing essential provisions. It was Friday, and I wasn't sure if the one supermarket on the island kept weekend hours, so I trekked back to Whitemark, getting to the store just before it closed at five thirty p.m.

There was a weekly barbecue in progress down on the dock. It was mostly attended by visitors to the island—a hardy-looking, weathered crew in fleeces and woolens. They'd come to bushwalk, kayak, and fish, since that's what there is to do here. They were clearly enjoying the salads and meats, all sourced from the island's farms. If I lived here, I would be friends with the young farmers who had produced this food, as I am with those on Martha's Vineyard. I suspected that it was the same mix: scions of multigenerational farming families and idealistic newcomers committed to organic and regenerative methods. One of the blessings of small places, especially islands: eventually you get to know everyone. You make friends with a far wider diversity of people than would ever happen in dense urban neighborhoods that are segregated by money and class.

It's windy but the rains have passed, and down by the Whitemark dock it's evident that the sunset will be a cracker. The conditions are perfect: clear horizon, but higher up, vast billows of cumulo-nimbus and cirrostratus clouds. The dock would be the perfect place to appreciate it, but I can't stay: the road is poor, and come dusk wildlife will be everywhere. I don't want to be responsible for one of the sad tangles of fur and bone smeared into the gravel. I will have to catch what I can of the show from the road.

Tony and I were connoisseurs of sunsets. Wednesday evenings, from early summer and into the Vineyard's mild fall, we'd gather with friends for a swim and a picnic on Lambert's Cove beach. It's a west-facing, white-sand crescent on the north shore of the island, easy swimming compared to the wilder ocean beaches to the south. The final event of the night was sunset-judging. We would award points from one to ten, and Tony would provide the commentary: "Only six? The Australian judge, notoriously harsh. Nine from the German judge? Officials suspect graft there. . . ."

Tony and I talked about how, in our old age, we would be sure to have a veranda facing west, equipped with a pair of rocking chairs. We would devote ourselves to watching sunsets, and never miss a good one.

But we were years from that, or so we thought. *Nel mezzo del cam-min di nostra vita*, in the middle of the journey of our lives, that's where we believed ourselves to be. Well past the Dantean age of thirty-five, to be sure, but still looking forward to a long and interesting road ahead. So much more work to do, so much more fun to have. Together. Instead, *mi ritrovai per una selva oscura*, and in that twilight forest I find myself all alone.

I don't know if the sunset turned out to be a ten. The shack faces east, with a bluff behind it, the western sky obscured. By the time I return, it's over.

At least I make it home without hitting a wombat.

The next morning it rains again, hard. The temperature is well below average for this time of year, so I decide to fire up the woodstove. I wish I'd thought to bring wood in, and now the pile is damp. It is a chore to get the stove going. There's no kindling, and it is too wet to gather any. I use the wax from a candle to ignite some old coals. When the rain lets up, I go for a quick walk on the beach, but it's raw, and I am glad to turn back toward the twirl of woodsmoke spiraling from the shack's chimney. A solitary pademelon has taken advantage of the break in the rain and is grazing right by the doorway. She turns her narrow face to me. I stop in my tracks, chastised. I'm the trespasser.

I am procrastinating. Fiddling with the woodstove, cooking up meals to sustain me in the days ahead—it is all a way of putting off what I have come here to do.

I must get on with the work.

May 28, 2019

CHEVY CHASE

As the sky lightened, I finally fell into a fitful doze. At one point I dreamed of Tony. He was present, alive. It was a warm, loving dream with no dark edges.

I woke out of it, and there was a minute or two when everything felt fine. He wasn't dead. How ridiculous to have thought that. Yesterday— that was the dream.

Then I came fully awake. I lost him a second time.

A restless night; an overwhelming day. Friends arrived with food. People asked about funeral arrangements. I didn't want anything to eat, and I didn't want to talk about funerals. I couldn't conceive of facing a horde of people, no matter how beloved. Tony's sister, Erica, became tearful when I said I couldn't imagine doing any- thing just yet. She said she couldn't just go home and go back to work as if nothing had happened. She is the older sister, always the mature presence around her baby brothers, an idealistic public defender, a tender mother, a sensitive soul. And my rabbi agreed with her on this. She gently suggested that our community at home yearned to express their grief, extend their condolences.

But how could I possibly think about venues, accommodations, catering platters? I couldn't. Not yet.

Obit writers called from *The New York Times, The Washington Post, The Wall Street Journal,* and *The Sydney Morning Herald.* Journalist friends at these newspapers stepped in and wrangled much of this, but there were questions I needed to answer.

I kept forgetting things. That Tony had recently been president of the Society of American Historians, a role he'd relished. Then one of the newspapers he had worked for. I had to keep calling back, emailing, correcting my errors. A reporter wanted to know Tony's graduation date from Brown. I didn't meet him till graduate school. I knew he'd taken time off in his junior year at college to work for the Frontier Nursing Service in Hyden, Kentucky, driving midwives into remote hollows to deliver care to some of the country's poorest people. So he hadn't graduated with his class. But when did he, actually?

Then his cardiologist called.

I badly wanted to speak to this man. I could barely bring myself to speak to him.

How had he let this happen?

Tony had a cardiologist because he suffered from hereditary hypertension and high cholesterol. He'd gone for a checkup just two months before he died. Even though he hated butter, cream, and fatty foods, and always declined dessert, he still needed statins and blood pressure meds. But so did his ninety-year-old mother, and we had no cause to believe that these issues wouldn't be as well managed for him as they had been for her. His first appointment with this doctor had been nine years earlier. He'd had a full workup and a stress test then, and nothing concerning had been flagged.

Now I learned that his recent visit hadn't been entirely routine. The cardiologist said Tony had come to see him complaining of shortness of breath. One time, as he ran for a train. And as the cardiologist related this, I remembered the incident. I recalled Tony, at the end of our last visit to DC at Passover, leaping from our Uber stuck in traffic, sprinting off in the direction of Union Station. He was late for the train to New York, where he had a meeting with his editor. Bizu and I were heading home by plane, and we smiled as we watched him, dodging and weaving through the cars, his wheelie bag held aloft above his head. No wonder he was short of breath when he fell into his seat on the Acela. Who wouldn't be?

But a few days later he'd found himself breathless again, during a game of tennis. He'd mentioned this to me in an offhand way. It seemed odd, he said, given that he worked out six days a week. Now, I learned from the cardiologist, Tony had been more worried about this than he had let on. Worried enough to take this concern to his doctor.

"It was a run-of-the-mill checkup. I didn't see any inflammation of the jugular, his EKG was unremarkable, his lungs were clear."

The doctor said he had tweaked Tony's meds and recommended a full workup, a battery of more definitive tests. But when they looked at the calendar of days left before his book tour, there was no one day on which all the necessary tests could be scheduled. Tony didn't want to give up the two full days it would take, schlepping back and forth to Boston. There was pre-publicity to do, decisions to be made about scheduling his time on the road—a million little things that seemed pressing. They'd settled on a date after the tour was over and made all the necessary appointments.

And there it was, inked in Tony's calendar: June 21 *MED TESTS*.

Twenty-five days too late. Why had they waited? Why this fatal delay?

I didn't know what to say to this doctor. I was afraid of what I might say. We agreed to speak again once he received the autopsy results. Weeks later, when I was scrolling nostalgically through Tony's tweets, I came across this one, from just after that March checkup:

> **Cardiologists are a hard-hearted lot. As one just told me: "I can give you a battery of tests, tell you all's fine, and the warranty on that is the time it takes you to get to the parking lot, where you could drop dead from a heart attack."**

Was that why he had felt a lack of urgency about those tests?

In the afternoon Bizu arrived with his aunt. In his mid-teens, he had a default demeanor that could best be described as defensive crouch, braced to swat away our stifling parental wing. A stoic kid who generally said a lot less than he thought, an unusual trait in a family of blabbermouths and oversharers.

My boy fell into my arms, weeping. We left the house and walked, hand in hand, to find the spot where Tony had collapsed. Josh's neighborhood is a long-settled place of mature trees, comfortable houses, and gardens riotous with spring bloom. We walked through dappled shade to Northampton Street. It wasn't far. We stood and stared at the commonplace squares of white concrete pavement. It was hard to fathom how something so shattering and consequential could have happened in such an ordinary spot.

"He loved you so much," I whispered. "He was so proud of you."

Bizu had thrived that year. He had chosen challenging classes and aced them. When Tony and I had recently visited his school, teachers had sought us out to praise him.

In her essay "On Grief" Jennifer Senior quotes a therapist who likens the survivors of loss to passengers on a plane that has crashed into a mountaintop and must find their way down. All have broken bones; none can assist the others. Each will have to make it down alone.

My sons' stories are their own to tell. I will not do that here. I will only say that on the street corner, with Bizu sagged against me, I did not know how lonely his journey would be and how little I would be able to help him.

When we got back to the house, there was a message from the DC medical examiner. They needed me to come downtown and identify Tony's body. This confused me, since they had said I couldn't see him till the autopsy was done and the body released to a funeral home.

"But how will I do an ID if I can't see his body?"

"You will do it from a photograph."

This isn't how it is supposed to happen. I had braced myself for metal drawers, tactful morgue attendants, the zip of a body bag. I was ready for that. Because at least it would be him. At least I would finally be beside him, able to touch him.

But even that small comfort was denied to me.

I made the appointment to do the ID. Friends who have friends in the DC bureaucracy arranged for a meeting with the medical examiner, to learn the findings of the autopsy. This was a great favor, for otherwise we'd have had to wait weeks for the report.

Josh and I went down together. A gleaming building, all glass and steel, just like any other DC office. No outward sign of the misery contained within. We passed through security and sat in a room with blond furnishings, like an upscale doctor's office. A young woman with Fulani braids and gel fingernails with stars embedded handed me a clipboard with a passport-sized photo, face down.

"When you're ready," she said, "you can turn it over and make the identification."

I would never be ready.

He looked terrible. He looked as if he had been through an ordeal. Which, of course, he had. But he was still Tony. I touched my hand to his face.

I'm sorry. Sorry I didn't take better care of you. Sorry I wasn't with you. Sorry I can't be with you now.

I *could* have been with him that Monday. Could have flown down to DC for the long weekend, gone with him to see the old friends in Waterford, walked with him to breakfast, held him in my arms as he died.

There were various reasons I had chosen not to go. We'd been together in Nashville the previous week, and a dear friend on the island was celebrating a big birthday. I was struggling to make headway on my novel, and Tony had been ribbing me about procrastinating: "*Horse* not exactly galloping to the finish line."

To top it off, travel to and from the island on Memorial Day was a massive headache, the only available flights inconvenient. So, I'd decided to stay put. It is a decision I will regret forever.

I made the ID and filled the forms the starry fingers placed in front of me. Then we waited for the medical examiner.

He was a trim man with a gentle demeanor, good at speaking about complicated things. Josh, who had been the point person for many family health crises, was particularly good at listening. Tony and I had relied on him when Nathaniel's birth had turned into an obstetrical emergency. Nathaniel, born with an Apgar score of one, had been whisked away by a crash team to the neonatal intensive care unit, our tiny infant hooked up to oxygen and IVs. Tony's dad had blamed us for having chosen a midwife to do the delivery instead of the ob-gyn he'd recommended. It was Josh who calmed him and got us all through it.

The medical examiner told us that he had initially thought Tony's cause of death was occlusion of the left anterior descending coronary artery. The body's biggest artery, the LAD supplies half of the heart muscle's blood supply. Like a criminal with a long rap sheet, this artery is the usual suspect in cases of sudden death like Tony's. It's known as the widow-maker. But the autopsy had revealed only 60 percent blockage in the LAD. Usually that degree of obstruction wouldn't even be an indicator for a stent. The examiner said he now thought Tony's arterial disease may have been incidental. He had another suspicion and to investigate it he had ordered microscopic sections, which would take some time to be prepared and evaluated.

So we still didn't know. But I was thankful for his care and his determination to arrive at an answer.

FLINDERS ISLAND

Unexpected visitors. I look up, and there is an elderly woman, leaning on a cane, making her slow way across my deck. It's startling. The few people I've seen out here have been specks in the far distance, way down the beach. Even more surprisingly she knocks, and when I open the door, she thrusts an empty shopping bag at me.

"I'm sorry I kept it so long."

"But it's not mine."

"Well, it belongs here." And off she goes.

I am still puzzling as to where she might have materialized from when Mick arrives, heralded by a glossy young kelpie and a senior-looking cattle dog. He is, he says, the farmer who owns the shack, and he's just come to check the gas bottles and the water tanks to make sure I don't run out.

He's a windswept blond with a deep farmer tan and has lived on the island for twenty years. I have a million questions I want to ask him, but he looks like a man with a lot to do, so I confine it to one: How is the island protecting itself from overdevelopment?

"People here are pretty unified about preserving it," he says. He explains that they're in a bit of a sweet spot with regards to tourism: "Airfare from Melbourne is six hundred twenty dollars, so that rules out hordes of backpackers, and the yuppies won't find any five-star accommodation here. They aren't gonna want a place like this," he says, spreading his hands to indicate the shack, ignoring the ridic-ulously glorious view of mountains and sea behind him. "It's got a loo out the back, right?" He grins conspiratorially. It does indeed have the loo out the back: a loo with a water view and a worn-out snorkel serving as the toilet roll holder.

I let Mick get about his chores and then happen to glance down at what I'm wearing. They're the same tatty shorts and old T-shirt I've been wearing every day. I run a hand through my hair. It's starched with unrinsed salt from ocean swimming. I would certainly never be mistaken for a yuppie. I hadn't noticed my appearance, since the mirror is in the outdoor shower, and I realize I haven't used it yet. It's been five days.

> *The mourner does not shave or cut his hair, nor does he bathe or shower for pleasure, during shivah. Laundering or wearing freshly laundered clothes is also proscribed. . . . It is a time-honored tra-dition to cover the mirrors.* ("Shiva and Other Mourning Obser-vances," Chabad.org.)

I have not intended to follow these strictures, but it seems I have.

Tony was a Jew, and I became one just before we married because I didn't want to be the end of an ancient lineage that had survived pogroms and the Shoah. Our kids went to Hebrew school, we observed Passover, High Holidays, Sukkot, Hanukkah, and sometimes a special meal and candles on Friday nights. But we weren't religious people, and our connection with the traditions was about culture and family. Had we been observant Jews, I would have had a road map through my grief, telling me exactly what to do and when to do it.

Orthodox Judaism divides mourning into phases. The most intense, *aninut*, is the time between the death and the burial. During *aninut*, grief is understood to be "stupefyingly intense." The mourner is not even to be offered condolences since she is not in any state to be consoled. Bystanders are supposed to quietly help in the practical matter of burial rites. During my *aninut* I was scrambling to get on boats and planes. I was arguing with hospital staff about seeing my husband's body, calling his publicist. My instinct to do these things, my conviction as to their necessity, had overridden any possibility of allowing my grief to be "stupefyingly intense."

After the burial, a Jewish mourner sits *shiva*. For seven days she stays home and essentially does nothing but accept condolence visits and reflect on the life of the lost person. A *minyan* (for the Orthodox, ten men) gathers daily with the bereaved to say *kaddish*, the death prayer that does not mention death. It is a time of complete withdrawal from the world and its demands. On the morning of the seventh day, one "gets up" from *shiva* and enters again into the routines of normal life. Traditionally friends accompany the mourner on a first walk outside the house. But for a further thirty days, or *sheloshim*, the mourner doesn't wear or buy new clothes, cut hair, listen to music, or take part in any celebrations. At the end of that thirty days, a spouse's mourning observance is considered to be over. Children are the only bereaved who are required to continue a full year of mourning rituals, for parents, on the basis that one may have multiple spouses, children, or siblings, but the bond with a parent is unique. (I am dismayed to learn that there is no obligation to mourn adoptive parents, only biological. It seems an unfair diminishment of parent, child, and the infinite capacity for love.)

Jews are expected to meticulously observe these requirements but not to exceed them. The idea is to provide an outlet for grief but also a framework to integrate the loss and move on with living.

While Jews limit the definition of mourners to a small number of close relationships (parents, children, spouses, siblings), Australia's First Nations people take a very different approach. In this fifty-thousand-year-old culture with the longest continuing religion in the world, mourning is understood to impact the entire community of the deceased. In traditional communities everyone is nominally related by assigned kinships that define rights, responsibilities, and even who may marry whom.

When someone dies, therefore, everyone who is part of that community takes part in rites known as Sorry Business, even if this means traveling a great distance. Each new arrival sets off another round of intense mourning. Ceremonies may last for weeks. "When a relation dies, we wait a long time with the sorrow," explains Miriam-Rose Ungunmerr-Baumann, an elder from the Northern Territory. "We own our grief and allow it to heal slowly." (Creative Spirits, "Sorry Business: Mourning an Aboriginal Death.")

In Islam a widow observes *iddah*, a three- or four-month partial withdrawal from the world. She can go to work and do necessary things, but she should not otherwise leave her home, dress up, or socialize. She may not enter into any agreement to marry during this time. I have read accounts by modern Muslim widows in favor of *iddah*, and those against it. One wrote about how it gave her the excuse she needed to be quiet and alone as well-intentioned friends were pressuring her to be social when she wasn't yet ready. Another noted feeling opprobrium if she so much as smiled or cracked a joke in public. She told an interviewer that she grieved and wept for her husband when she was in private. She did not need to be told how or when to mourn him.

Most faith traditions put guardrails up around the bereaved, rules for what to do in those days of massive confusion when the world has collapsed. In Islam there are specific observances for the third, seventh, and fortieth days after burial. As a reporter in Tehran I attended a *shab-e haft*, or seventh-night service, for a ninety-year-old matriarch. I sat in my black chador in the women's courtyard. From the neighbor's house, where the men had gathered, a mullah with a mellifluous voice intoned verses from the Koran and then sang a long and mournful song extolling the virtues of mothers. This was piped to our gathering via a loudspeaker strung up on the courtyard's boundary wall.

The women wept. The tears weren't necessarily only for the deceased. These women had plenty to cry about. In this one courtyard were mothers who had lost sons in the long war with Iraq, a mother who had seen a son executed for joining an anti-revolutionary terrorist group, and a young woman who had just been released from seven years as a political prisoner for shouting "Death to Khomeini!" Here was a place to express grief openly, no matter one's political opinions.

A year or so earlier I had reported on the funeral for Ayatollah Khomeini. From the Huey helicopter that carried reporters to the grave site, I could see that the city's roads had become rivers of black—black-clad mourners, marching southward to the burial place down every major road, every alleyway, chanting prayers, wailing, beating their breasts and their brows until, sometimes, they bled. Forty days later I was invited back to Tehran as the entire country observed *chehelom*, or the fortieth day after his funeral. On that occasion one mourns again as intensely as if it is the first day. But the day after, life returns to normal. In Tehran all the black banners would be removed from public places, and people would no longer be expected to wear black clothing. No matter the eminence of the deceased person or the intensity of the grief, Islamic mourning had an understood end point.

The service I attended was held in a sports arena, and I kept my pass for the Khomeini family women's section in my wallet for years. It might, I thought, be my get-out-of-basement-free card, if I ever found myself taken hostage by certain extremist groups.

For Filipino Catholics the ninth day after death is significant: mourners gather once again to pray. Hindus, after a cremation, mourn intensely for thirteen days. Mourners are considered unclean and must avoid sacred spaces and adhere to other taboos that set the mourning period apart from ordinary life. For Buddhists, ceremonies and prayers for the dead are conducted every seven days for seven weeks. After the ceremony on the forty-ninth day, the spirit of the deceased is thought to move on to its next incarnation.

In Bali's Hindu and animist traditions, bodies are buried for as long as it takes to gather the necessary resources for the elaborate cremation ritual needed to move the spirit from this life to the next. Wives have many exacting ceremonial duties to perform, but they do these things surrounded by family and community, a constant reminder that while one pillar of their life has been taken, many other ties of affection remain. By the time the colorful procession takes place to the cremation site, sometimes weeks or months later, the mood is no longer somber, but light, a celebration of the soul becoming free.

In her memoir *Fragrant Rice,* Janet De Neefe explains how Balinese beliefs ameliorate the sting of death's finality. She writes of how her first baby, Dewi, was deemed to be the reincarnation of her husband's late mother. As soon as a priest had made that pronouncement, the woman's elderly friends arrived, cradling the baby, calling her by her former name, chatting to her of how they had missed her and catching her up on their doings since her death.

Tony didn't believe in an afterlife, and certainly not in reincarnation. He believed that death was the end. I believe that, too. Nevertheless, things have occurred in the aftermath of his passing that I cannot explain.

Just after he died, one of his cousins reached out to me. For years this young woman had been estranged from most of the family, but she had reconnected warmly with Tony at one of his last book readings near her home on the West Coast. She emailed to say she had consulted her psychic, who had a vision of Tony on the edge of a cliff surrounded by masses of yellow and red flowers, so she had planted a memorial garden for him at her home, with flowers in those colors. How nice, I replied, and didn't think anything more of it.

The next spring, exactly a year after his death, just as I became aware that I had lived through all four seasons without him, a mass of tulips appeared in my own garden. Lipstick red, chrome yellow; others with glossy petals of variegated red and yellow. I hadn't planted them: I never plant tulips since squirrels too often eat the bulbs. And I'd designed that border with plants only in white and soft shades of lilac. Yet there they are, spring following spring, bright red and vivid yellow tulips as glaring as traffic lights. Inexplicable.

I know that Tony would scoff. And he would probably disapprove of this urge I have, here on Flinders, to make up my own mourning ritual. At least he would find something mocking to say about it.

I see myself as he would see me, disheveled and alone, washed up on a beach at the ends of the earth, observing memorial days of no fixed duration. I can see him grinning, amused. "What do you think you're doing, you mad woman? For god's sake, go to the pub!"

I smile back at him, but I shake my head. I'm allowing myself, at last, to wait a long time with my sorrow.

To wait with it as long as it takes.

Chevy Chase

That first day without him felt interminable. It finally drew to a close on a surreal note.

Tony had recorded an interview for *PBS NewsHour* the day after his book was published. He'd hoped, as all authors do, that it would air in that fleeting moment when publishers have paid booksellers to keep copies front and center in bookstores—the valuable real estate of the New Release table. As the days passed after the recording, Tony had been anxious. He knew very well that the pressure of breaking news meant that soft features like book interviews, without an obvious news peg, might languish unaired for weeks.

His death was a news peg. We all gathered in Josh and Ericka's den, in front of their large TV. The screen filled with Tony's author photo, taken in our paddock with one of our huge-eyed alpacas gazing over his shoulder. Across the bottom of the screen, like an engraving on a tombstone:

TONY HORWITZ
1958–2019

"Finally, tonight we remember and hear from author and Pulitzer Prize–winning journalist Tony Horwitz," said Judy Woodruff. "He died suddenly yesterday of an apparent cardiac arrest. Horwitz was best known as the author of *Confederates in the Attic*, a look at modern-day Southern attitudes about the Civil War and the people who reenact it. The book was a bestseller. As a journalist he covered conflicts in Africa, the Middle East, and the Balkans for *The Wall Street Journal*. He won the Pulitzer in 1995 for a series on income inequality and low-wage jobs, including working in chicken-processing plants in the South. A number of Horwitz's books are told through the narrative of first-person account. That's true of his latest book, *Spying on the South*. William Brangham recently sat down with him about it. Here's that interview. . . ."

It was almost wonderful, seeing him: handsome, animated. For a minute I forgot the circumstances, lost in the pleasure of watching him. He was good at this: talking in sound bites, hitting the book's best anecdotes. He told how he had reconnected with an old college text, *The Cotton Kingdom* by Frederick Law Olmsted, while trying to cull the overflowing bookshelves in our barn. Olmsted, many years before he found his métier as the designer of Central Park and other iconic landscapes, had been a reporter for *The New*

York Times, sent south in the years before the Civil War to probe the nation's growing divisions. Tony recounted how he was struck by the similarities with this present moment of American fracture, and how he had decided to retrace Olmsted's journeys, comparing what Fred had seen then with what he found now.

It was an inspired idea, especially since Fred and Tony had such a similar approach to reporting: Don't go to big shots and experts. Report from the ground up, hang out with regular people, ask them about their lives. Explore important issues while also finding the humor in everyday predicaments. It had made a brilliant book.

But at what cost. Tony drove himself to exhaustion reporting it. He had always pushed to the limit; that was nothing new. But the older he got, the harder he found it to sustain the manic energy it took to convince strangers to let him work beside them on a coal barge on the Ohio River, to party with monster-truck lovers at a debauch called Mudfest in Louisiana, or to travel through Hill Country Texas on muleback. Tony's mule wound up giving him a concussion that landed him in the ER and messed him up for a month. Of course, he turned even that unpleasant episode into a funny, self-deprecating chapter, embracing the title "Rhinestone Jewboy."

Then there was the writing, always an intense thing for Tony but this time ramped up by a pressing publishing schedule and a tight deadline. To get the book done on time, he chewed boxes of Nicorette gum; nibbled Provigil, the pill developed to keep fighter pilots alert; drank pints of coffee. Thus wired he'd write till mid-afternoon, then go to the gym for an hour, crush the StairMaster, pump iron. Come home, chew more Nicorette, and put in another hour or two.

At night he countered all the stimulants with wine. This put him to sleep, but then woke him in the wee hours. At which point he'd get up, answer all the emails he hadn't had time for during the day, and drink more wine.

So much wine.

If anyone in our household was going to have a drinking problem, it was likely going to be me. In my family tree drunks swung from every branch. My father was an alcoholic. So were both his parents. My mother didn't drink, but *her* mother drank too much, and more than once we'd come home to find my mum's uncle Oscar passed out on the front veranda, aromatic as a brewery. I started drinking at university to overcome a crushing shyness, then went to work as a reporter at a time when Sydney newsrooms floated on a sea of booze. But as I gained confidence, I relied less on drink, and then moving to the United States and the more abstemious newsroom culture of *The Wall Street Journal* further interrupted my slide into dissipation. That, and the example of my family. None of them was a fun drunk. My lovely dad and my sweet grandmother could become mean, even monstrous, in drink.

Tony was different. As an undergrad in the early eighties, he'd indulged in the degeneracies of the era—too much drinking and too many psychedelics, until a bad trip scared him off. By the time I

met him he'd toned down the excess and was merely an ebullient
social drinker. In thirty-five years, I could count on one hand the
times I'd seen him messily intoxicated.

When we lived in Cairo, it was possible for us, as foreigners, to buy
liquor, but it required reams of paperwork and wasn't worth the
bother. In our rare downtime between assignments, we'd sit in the
dining room of our hot apartment—the AC never quite worked—
and play endless hands of Basra, a fast-paced card game Tony had
learned in an Iraqi coffee shop. Occasionally we'd share a single
bottle of soapy Egyptian beer. When we had to go entirely without,
reporting in dry countries such as Saudi Arabia, Libya, and Iran, it
wasn't a problem.

We were less abstemious in Sydney and London, where the drinking culture leads easily to intemperance. But it was something you
did on weekends, at a table surrounded by friends. It was a fun release, not a daily habit, not an ardent need.

During the writing and reporting of his last book, that changed. He
lost the off switch with his drinking. He would go until the bottle
stood empty. I started watching him at social events, making sure
we left the party before he overdid it.

He knew this was unsustainable. He would bring it to a halt, he said,
for sure. After the book tour. No more booze, pills, Nicorette. He
would detox, reset his system. He realized he might need help, so he
sought advice from friends who'd gone on the wagon and from his

cardiologist on how to taper the drinking. We brainstormed about a next project that wouldn't require the same kind of high-stress mental and physical mania.

I looked forward to the day this new leaf was to be turned over. I began researching spas. After his book tour we'd go away together. We'd spend three weeks, maybe a month, with no booze, eating raw veggies. We'd hike up mountains, swim. Maybe even do yoga. We'd come home with new habits. Our next-door neighbor was a talented yoga teacher, her airy studio right across the field from our house. Maybe we'd turn into one of those radiant older couples with yoga mats under their arms and serene smiles on their faces.

All this would happen. We just had to get through the book tour.

FLINDERS ISLAND

I wake before dawn and watch the sunrise silvering the concave curves of the clouds and then turning them roseate, strewing the sky with pink petals.

I have decided to leave the shack today and go back to Wybalenna. It was one of the places on this island that Tony and I visited together when we came here in 2000, when I was doing research for the novel I then intended to write.

After our son Nathaniel was born in 1996, I no longer wanted to go off on long, open-ended newspaper assignments to dangerous places. It was Tony who convinced me to try to write fiction. I was a reporter to my core. It was what I had wanted to do for most of my life. I had learned to be good at it. I had zero confidence I'd be any good at making things up. But Tony encouraged me to try, and so I wrote my first novel, *Year of Wonders*. When we made the trip to Flinders, that book was about to be published, and my editor had encouraged me to propose another.

I decided that my second novel would be based on the life of Jane Franklin, an English silk merchant's daughter who came to Tasmania in 1837 as wife of the governor. Tasmania was then the penal colony of last resort for convicts who re-offended after transportation to Sydney. It was a place where cruelty was magnified and radiated, notorious for the worst brutalities to Indigenous people, who were hunted and slaughtered, the few survivors exiled to Flinders Island. Jane Franklin's tenacious campaigning against these cruelties ultimately led to her husband's recall.

I had learned about Jane in my early years as a reporter, covering environmental issues for *The Sydney Morning Herald*. Along with politicians and conservationists I'd rafted down the river named after her husband, the Franklin, wild and scenic from source to mouth, and at that time at risk of being dammed for a nugatory amount of hydroelectric power.

The river rushed through true wilderness: old-growth rainforest thick with horizontal scrub, resistant to human penetration. It was a demanding trip for a city person who didn't know from camping. We were each in our own small inflatable raft, and I learned to paddle for my life over roaring rapids and portage my gear across steep, slippery riverbanks. I slept in a tent sagging under torrential rain, smelled like a wet sheep in my army-surplus woolens, ached in muscles I hadn't even known I had.

It was a life-altering journey. For the first time I experienced a place where nature is big and we are small. I understood that wilderness was what my human brain and body had been adapted to for millennia and that the only life I'd known, in a crowded city, was a profoundly unnatural habitat for my species.

One evening, as we camped below the majestic Rock Island Bend, one of the conservationists emerged from the rainforest with a fistful of foliage. "I thought you might like to know what the trees are," he said, turning over the delicate fronds of a Huon pine, the serrated leaves of a celery top, the glossy blade of a laurel. I had been looking at these same trees for days without really differentiating them. Suddenly I could see my surroundings with new clarity.

I fell in love with Tasmania's wild places and the young activists fighting to save it. I started to think about moving there, giving up the objectivity of journalism, becoming a wilderness campaigner, helping to build the country's nascent Green Party. And then I learned I had won the Greg Shackleton scholarship to Columbia University, named for a brave young correspondent murdered by the Indonesian army while covering the invasion of East Timor.

The campaign against the Franklin dam was reaching a climax. I was reluctant to leave the story behind as thousands organized to blockade the dam site. But Columbia, a master's degree, a New York adventure tempted me. It was my sliding-door moment: foreign correspondent or Tasmanian conservationist? In the end I took the scholarship, met Tony, got hired by *The Wall Street Journal*, led an entirely different life.

But Tasmania's wild landscapes and Jane Franklin's story had stayed with me. Within the constraints of the Georgian era, Jane had lived a large life, becoming the most widely traveled woman of her generation. She scandalized the colony when she explored the Franklin River region in the company of convict porters. I was drawn to her adventurous spirit and to her activism on behalf of women prisoners and Aboriginal people.

So, on a blustery morning, Tony and I had set out from our bed-and-breakfast headed for Wybalenna, a place central to her story. In our years as foreign correspondents, based in Cairo and London, we'd often reported together, no matter whose byline wound up on the final article. We were each other's second pair of eyes and ears, as symbiotic in our working life as that fungus and algae together making the vivid orange *Caloplaca*. By the end of our careers at *The Wall Street Journal*, editors began to refer to us in news meetings as Hobro, and that was how we increasingly saw ourselves. Beyond partners, essentially one person.

We maintained this symbiosis as book writers, bouncing ideas off each other, reading each other's drafts, trading skills. I benefited from Tony's knack for archive diving and his ruthless editing. He would find my favorite words and kill them off with a pen slash. He had it in, especially, for two adjectives I overused: "desiccated" and "gnarled." They kept creeping into my prose; he kept tossing them out.

For my part I could assist him in portraying the natural world with more specificity than his go-to descriptors: "bush," "flower," "tree." Sometimes I suggested a useful narrative direction or an avenue of inquiry that he hadn't thought of. Whenever we could, we accompanied each other on research trips—a second pair of ears and eyes hoovering up detail. That's why he came with me to Wybalenna.

There are many places where Aboriginal people fought to the death, spears against guns, defending their lands. I am not sure there is another place as haunted as Wybalenna.

This was a massacre in slow motion, where people died in forced exile. When Aborigines evaded capture on the Tasmanian mainland, a tactic was to kidnap their children, saying they would be returned to them only when the parents went to Flinders Island. After years of resistance, one chief capitulated when his daughter was stolen. She was never returned to him and died in an orphanage in Hobart. He and his wife later had another daughter, Mathinna, before they, too, died at Wybalenna of disease and despair.

The settlement name means "Black People's Houses," and when Jane Franklin visited Wybalenna, there was a row of twenty dwellings, pressed together like a London slum, incongruous on this windswept expanse of coastal heathland. After her second visit she sent for the six-year-old child she had met there, Mathinna. Taken from whatever relatives she still had, delivered to Government House in Hobart, Mathinna was raised with the Franklins' seventeen-year-old daughter, Eleanor. Dressed up in a puff-sleeved red gown, driven around in the viceregal carriage, required to sit for a portrait, the child seems to have been, for a time, a full member of the family. In a poignant letter Mathinna wrote: "I am a good little girl, I have pen & ink cause I am good little girl. I do love my father. I have got a doll & shift & petticoat. . . . I have got red frock. . . . I have got sore feet & shoes & stockings & I am very glad."

In 1843, when John Franklin was recalled to England, Jane Franklin abandoned Mathinna at the same orphanage in Hobart where her older sister had perished. Jane did this knowing the place was crowded and disease-ridden, a place of hunger and harsh punishments. She didn't even leave the girl her doll. (It recently turned up in an English museum, bequeathed by a descendent of Eleanor's.) When Mathinna couldn't adjust, she was shipped back to Flinders Island, and when that hopeless settlement was entirely abandoned, she went with the handful of survivors to another place of destitution near Hobart. She drowned there, aged twenty. There is no evidence that Jane Franklin ever inquired about her.

There's one thing you must be able to do as a novelist, and that is understand how your characters explain their own actions to themselves. No amount of thinking could provide me with the story Jane Franklin had told herself to justify abandoning that child. And because I could not access her thoughts, I eventually concluded that I couldn't write a novel about her.

On that first visit to Wybalenna with Tony, I was only beginning to grasp the edges of the story. As we walked the windy field of gently sloping grasslands, I noticed drifts of miniature iris blooming between the settlement chapel and the superintendent's house. It was an English flower, not native. I dug up a corm, wrapped it in damp tissue, and carried it home to plant in my garden in Sydney.

I imagined a nineteenth-century superintendent's wife doing the same, digging up corms of her favorite iris in her English garden and carrying them across the sea to Tasmania. Perhaps she was optimistic about the journey, looking forward to the garden she would make. Perhaps she was afraid. I don't believe she could have imagined the misery she would witness.

In my Sydney garden, when the iris bloomed the following spring, I reminded Tony of our trip to Flinders Island. "It's so beautiful there, and the land's still cheap. I'd love to save up and buy a block one day." He grunted, noncommittal, and quickly changed the subject.

There are no irises in bloom when I visit this time. It's too late in the summer. The fields stretch away in pale golden hues of sun-bleached grass. I walk to the cemetery where many Aboriginal people lie, their graves unmarked. But there is a marker for Elizabeth Milligan, wife of the superintendent, dead at nineteen, "one day after her confinement."

If the intention is mourning, I have come to the right place.

Chevy Chase

The medical examiner finally released Tony's body to the funeral director. Josh had retained the small, no-frills funeral business his father, a pragmatist, selected before his own death in 2012. Josh's wife had also chosen it for her father when he died five years later at the age of eighty-six.

Tony's father was eighty-seven when he died of complications from Parkinson's disease. Tony's mother was ninety and still active. How much faith has been mistakenly placed in the longevity of these parents! Long-lived parents beget long-lived offspring, or so we believed. Dr. Norman Horwitz removed brain tumors and extracted bullets from spines until he was seventy. He survived a dissected aorta and continued consulting on difficult cases at Walter Reed National Military Medical Center till the very last months of his life. How dismayed Norman would be to know his youngest child had twenty-seven years less life than he did.

The funeral parlor is not the sort of place that has ornate chapels. They don't, strictly speaking, even have a viewing room. People who choose their stripped-down services don't usually want that. But Josh has explained our situation, and they have told him we can stop by in the late afternoon.

Bizu, beside me most of the day, had been visibly distressed by the press of people, the noisy chatter, the sharing of stories about Tony. When the stories were funny ones, which was often, he winced at the laughter. He was plainly not ready for this. I needed to get him home. Nathaniel was once again in flight—fifteen hours from Sydney to Dallas, then four more to Boston, then the forty-five-minute puddle jumper to the Vineyard. I booked an evening flight so we could be home before he arrived. We would visit the funeral home on the way to the airport.

It was a nondescript storefront in a nondescript strip mall. I asked Bizu if he was sure about his decision not to come inside, then gave him a hug and left him to wait in the car. A tiny office, a young woman behind the desk. Josh had met her before when he dealt with the cremations of his dad and his father-in-law. She was gentle and sincere, apologizing for the cramped space as she ushered us into a small room tucked behind the office.

And there he was. Wrapped up in a soft white blanket, only his face showing, his head deeply cushioned. Later, when I read the autopsy report, I realized that this was to hide the medical violence that had been done to him. But I was glad to finally see his face.

I stroked his cheek. It was cool, as if he'd just come out of the ocean after a sunset swim. His hair was still faintly damp from the washing of his body. He no longer looked thrashed and haggard, as he had in the morgue photo. He looked exactly like himself, a handsome and contented man in the prime of middle age. And that, now, was what he would remain.

"My love," I kept repeating. "My love." I needed to hold his hand, but when I reached for the edge of the white blanket, the woman stopped me. "Just let me get him ready for that," she said. Josh and I stepped out for a moment. In truth, I would have been glad to see it all—the autopsy incisions, everything—but I was not in any condition to resist her kind intentions.

I've always loved his hands. Big, meaty, peasant's hands. His touch, insistent with desire. The weight of his arm flung over me before we fell asleep.

I held his hand. I didn't want to ever let it go.

FLINDERS ISLAND

Wallowing. Is that what this is?

My mother was a great foe of wallowing. *Get over yourself. Think about other people for a change.* She didn't entertain self-pity, though many facts of her life would have allowed for it. In Gloria's world, you got on with it. Her empathy was vast, her activism relentless. You did everything you could about what you could change. You didn't sit around crying over what you could not.

As I child I was strenuously encouraged to save my tears. Weeping over books or films was disapproved of. When I was about seven, the neighbors took me to the drive-in to see the Disney movie *The Three Lives of Thomasina*, in which a distressing number of grim fates befall endearing animals. When I came home, snotty and red-eyed, I lied and said my eyes were watery because the neighbors had been smoking in the car. Among the cherished freedoms of my adult life was the freedom to cry whenever I wanted to: at soppy movies, books, poems, even, god help me, Telstra ads. My sister joked that I teared up at the weather report.

Once, years into my career as a foreign correspondent, I was driving through Hebron on the West Bank just as school let out. I was in an Israeli rental car with non-Palestinian plates, so I had a Palestinian keffiyeh on my dashboard and the Arabic word for "journalist" written on my windshield to differentiate me from an Israeli settler. But it was a rookie mistake to drive past a school at that hour, and when the *shebab*—the young boys—swarmed my car and started hurling stones and chunks of concrete, I swore at myself for blundering into such a predictable situation. The windshield shattered, the metal crunched. Another second and one of those chunks of rock might smash my skull. Knowing it was my only choice, I jumped out and yelled at the kids.

"Leish, kidda? Anna sahafiyya!" Why in the world? I am a reporter!

From nearby houses adults emerged, shouting angrily at the boys, who quickly dispersed, looking sheepish.

The adults took me inside, handed me tea. Shock set in, I suppose, and I began sobbing. Big heaving sobs that came up from a deep place in my gut and made me shake from head to toe. We use the word "hysterical" loosely, but this was the real thing. I tried to stop, to compose myself, vexed at my loss of control, embarrassed in front of people who lived under military occupation and alongside some of the most extremist Israeli settlers. My hosts had undoubtedly been through much more terrifying experiences than mine. But that day my body demanded its release.

I haven't cried like that for Tony. I should have, the moment I received the news of his death. But I was afraid to give way to it. Remembering that day in Hebron, that complete lack of self-control, I knew that if I started, I mightn't be able to stop. So I shut it down. And for the past two years, I haven't been able to cry at all.

As I drove away from Wybalenna yesterday, I did as my mother had instructed: I thought about other people. Specifically, the miserable fate of the kidnapped women, the exiled men, the children, stolen and then abandoned. The brokenhearted people looking across the narrow strait separating them from the sustaining lands they loved. I still had so much; they had been left with nothing.

People die. On the descent to JFK Airport one day after Tony's death, I stared from my airplane window at the close-pressed houses of the Queens borough, thinking: I have this in common with every single one of all the thousands of people down there, living their varied, vivid lives. We might have not one other single thing in common, but we've got this. We will all die. We will all grieve. Women lose their husbands. Widows, widows everywhere. Two of my close friends had lost husbands to cancer, and another, suddenly, to stroke. Almost exactly two years to the day that I got the shattering news about Tony, a text appeared on my phone announcing another shocking death. My goddaughter, a fierce and radiant nineteen-year-old, had been killed in a car crash. The theft of her life seemed like a blow no parent, no sibling could recover from.

And yet here I was, wallowing.

Absent-mindedly I turned on the car radio. I hadn't listened to any news all week. An intentional part of my retreat from the world was shutting out the usual noises, and news is my habitual background noise. At home I live with a soundtrack of National Public Radio and the BBC. Mary Louise Kelly and James Coomarasamy might as well be my roommates. The radio is generally on in the kitchen and in the car, so I can catch headlines while running errands, grabbing coffee, cooking.

"The death toll from the massive earthquake in Türkiye and Syria is one thousand five hundred and is expected to rise as rescuers sift through rubble in a race against the cold . . ."

Soon, that death toll rose to twenty-six hundred. A few hours after that, it was more than thirty-five hundred.

They die all through that day. They die, trapped in the rubble as the snow falls. They die waiting to be triaged, freezing outside hospitals that have no beds. "It's not normal triage," the hospital's only doctor tells the reporter. "I can't choose the ones I might save. I can only choose the ones I might save who won't need too many resources. We just don't have them."

While I have a long swim on this beautiful, empty beach, they are dying. As I sit in the sun drying off, they are dying. By the time I go to bed, the death toll is five thousand. An official from the Red Crescent blurts that the final number will likely be twenty thousand. Soon it is thirty-three thousand. In the end it will be close to sixty thousand souls.

I know that area of Türkiye. Tony and I both reported from the Kurdish city Diyarbakır, not far from the epicenter. It was a restive place, caught between the hammer of the Turkish military and the anvil of a radical separatist movement. Later it became a jumping-off place for trips into Kurdish Iraq after the first Gulf War. As a reporter covering catastrophes, I had always tried to find the individual in the big number, the one person whose story, whose individual pain, a reader could relate to.

As I listen to the radio, a reporter does this. He describes a distraught father, sitting in rubble, holding the hand of his dead fifteen-year-old daughter. It is the only part of her he can touch. The rest is crushed under collapsed concrete slabs.

Another reporter interviews a young man as he claws through ice-rimed rubble, trying to dig down to the ruins of the kitchen in which he knows his mother is trapped. He fears she is dead, even as he must hope she is alive. "Everybody wants to die normally, you know?"

How can I mourn my one loss amid such an abundance of death? My one man, who I have reason to believe did not suffer at his ending.

He dropped dead. That quotidian phrase so carelessly tossed off before it had a particular, personal meaning.

Everybody wants to die normally, you know.

But not so soon. Not so soon.

May 29, 2019

BWI AIRPORT

When Bizu and I arrived at Baltimore airport, I went to the newsstand and got copies of *The Wall Street Journal, The Washington Post, The New York Times*. We read the obituaries, passing the papers from hand to hand.

> The *Journal*'s obituary said Tony was *"among the most talented and dogged reporters on the staff . . . an amiable genius—the best combination of bulldog reporter and transcendent writer."*

> The *Times* quoted David Blight, a historian Tony venerated: *"Tony created his own unique genre of history and journalism. . . . His search for Olmsted's journey was Tony's own brilliant mirror held up to all of us about the awful social and political sicknesses we face now as Olmsted's*

*epic journey showed the same for the South and the road
to the Civil War."*

In the *Post*: *"He was often in situations that could be considered comical, if they weren't so dangerous. In the middle of a demonstration in Tehran, Mr. Horwitz found
himself in a crowd chanting 'Death to America.' He met an
English-speaking demonstrator who unexpectedly asked
Mr. Horwitz about Disneyland. 'It has always been my
dream,' he said, 'to go there and take my children on the
tea-cup ride.' Then the protester resumed shouting 'Death
to America!' Another time, Mr. Horwitz was under siege
from artillery fire in a boat outside Beirut, when a fellow
passenger turned to him and said, 'You are very brave. And
maybe very stupid.'"*

There is consolation in this. These long obituaries give a detailed
account of the work that he cared for and vivid glimpses of his personality. There is more. Both local papers on the Vineyard run
obits, one with a headline he would have loved: *Tony Horwitz,
Author, Historian, Regular Island Guy.*

The comments on the websites of both papers contain an outpour-
ing of love and reminiscence from our neighbors. *The Sydney Morning Herald*, where he worked when we lived in Australia, ran an
affectionate memoir by his mate Andrew Denton, who traveled with
him for part of the reporting for *Spying on the South* and appears as
a sidekick in one of the book's funniest sections. On NPR Terry
Gross reran both the interview she did with him for *Confederates in*

the Attic and critic Maureen Corrigan's glowing review of *Spying on the South*, which had first aired the previous week, when Tony was still alive to enjoy it. *The New Yorker*, where he worked briefly as a staff writer, had a perceptive appreciation by Jill Lepore. He would have blushed to read her description of him: "A distinguished American historian with a singular voice, full of compassion and delight and wry observations and self-deprecating humor—layers that covered but never obscured his deep and abiding moral seriousness about the task of the historian as the conscience of a nation."

And even as I write this, I feel Tony's disapprobation. I see his pen slashes, his terse scrawl: *Cut this. Bragging.*

But I will not. For even sitting there at the airport, wrapped in sadness, I knew to be thankful for these obituaries. They reminded me how much life Tony had packed into his sixty years, and how easily it could have ended sooner if any one of the crazy risks we took in our reporting years had gone the wrong way. I also felt anguish for all the people who had suffered losses on this day whose beloveds' quirks and jokes and accomplishments would never be publicly noted. Whose sons would not be able to read about their father and know how he was appreciated and loved, even by strangers.

I resolved to remember this as we face what's coming. I resolved to be grateful.

FLINDERS ISLAND

My Potemkin Personality. The phrase comes to me as I am walking the beach this afternoon.

I have erected a facade that I have hidden behind, a fugitive from my own feelings. It's heavy and elaborate and it's taken a lot of energy to haul it around with me every time I leave the house. Especially this past year, when I have been so much in the world, on a book tour myself. ("Don't die, Mum," said Nathaniel, as I left for the airport on the day before my novel's publication, heading to Tennessee for my first event.)

It was the tour for *Horse*, the novel that Tony believed in more than I did. The book he didn't let me give up on even when I was ready to abandon it, overwhelmed by the unique challenges it posed. The book I dragged myself back to my desk to finish, only so that I could dedicate it to him. The book that now seems as if it might be the one that readers like best of all.

My first event on that tour, on the day the novel came out, was at Parnassus Books in Nashville. It's a store that belongs to a writer I admire, a person I love. I first met Ann Patchett glancingly at an awards event where *Year of Wonders* was short-listed but *Bel Canto* deservedly won. I met her properly in 2015 in Nashville, in the back room of her bookstore where she had come to chat with me as I signed a tower of copies of *The Secret Chord*, which she had chosen for her First Editions book club. I loved the bookstore on first sight, because it was full of dogs. Ann, like me, is a dog obsessive, and her staff are encouraged to bring their dogs to work.

"I'm one dog away from being shut down by the health department," she said, as I patted her personality-packed dog Sparky and admired Mary Todd Lincoln, a demure miniature dachshund who traveled the world in a baby sling.

"So," she said. "I don't know anything about your life. Tell me."

"Well, you know I'm married to Tony Horwitz. . . ."

"No!" she exclaimed. "How's that working out for you?"

Tony had a certain notoriety in literary Nashville. The first time he'd given a talk there, for *Confederates in the Attic*, it had been disrupted by white supremacists—oh, excuse me, "heritage groups"— and police had been called. The so-called heritage guys somewhat gave the game away when they called the Black cop who arrived the N-word.

I allowed as how marriage to Tony was working out well, since by then we'd been married thirty-one years.

Ann is both empathetic and acerbic, a combination that reminds me of my mum. When her novel *Commonwealth* came out, I persuaded her to present it at the Martha's Vineyard book festival so that we could hang out together. She and her husband, Karl, a chevalier from Mississippi, stayed with us.

And now we shared a strange bond. The very last time Tony and I were together was in Nashville. I'd joined him a week into his book tour. The events manager at Parnassus thought it would be fun if I interviewed him, and I jumped at the chance to join him on the road and reconnect with Ann.

The last meal we'd had together was after that event, with Ann and Bruce, Tony's roommate when we were grad students together at Columbia Journalism School. Bruce, a southerner, had settled in Nashville, in a house just a few doors down from Ann's.

It had been a lovely day. Tony had just come from a packed event at the Jimmy Carter Presidential Library in Atlanta. Ann had chosen his book for her First Editions Club, which puts a title on the runway to the bestseller list. That afternoon I sat in the back room of her store, pushing books over to Tony as he signed them, chatting to Ann and her talented staff. When we were done with the signing, there was only about an hour till the event, so Tony and I went for a quiet drink at a little bar nearby and caught each other up on the small and large doings of our week apart.

At the end of the event, Tony signed more books, engaging everyone who wanted to chat. I remember being impatient to get to dinner, but quelling the feeling, knowing that this was part of Tony's gift—his ability to form connections, his completely sincere interest in other people. After dinner we retreated to our hotel and wrapped ourselves in the warm love of bodies long familiar with each other.

In the morning Tony was driving to Louisville, for what he already knew would be a full house at the Filson Historical Society, and I was flying home. (The next morning he emailed me that Louisville had been a great success: a crowd of eight hundred, many books signed. "Only glitch, I forgot to turn off my phone and it rang in middle of talk in my shoulder bag in front row, so shlepper had to dig thru Nicorette and bloody tissues (cut myself shaving) to turn it off. just checked and it appears to be a butt dial from you.")

When we'd last been together, a week earlier in New York City, we'd met up with old friends and celebrated his book's publication day at the restaurant named Olmsted in Brooklyn. Knowing how rigorous his coming week would be, I'd crept out of the hotel the next morning without waking him, without saying goodbye.

But that morning in Nashville we said a proper farewell. "I can't believe it's ten days before I'll see you again." I am certain he is the one who said it; he always had a clearer calendar in his head than I. But it might as well have been me. We both felt it. That morning we were as much in love as we had ever been. We were looking forward to life after book tour and all the good things that would happen then. A long kiss, and I left in a cab for the airport.

One of my friends told me her sister has had to live with her last words to her husband on the day he died suddenly: "I can't believe you forgot to get gas."

I can't believe it's ten days before I'll see you again.

I can't believe I will never see you again.

I will always wish I had made a different decision and met him in Washington the following week. But I am glad, at least, to have had that last day together, those parting words.

WEST TISBURY

Bizu and I stepped off the ferry into torrential chilly rain, the kind of dispiriting late May reversal all too characteristic of Vineyard spring. Salem, Bizu's godmother, gathered us up and drove us home. We live about twenty minutes' drive from the ferry dock, an area of farms and woods with a tiny town center that consists of a general store, a town hall, a white clapboard church, and a library. We were lucky to find this old millhouse, the rare Vineyard home that satisfied both my urge for a rural life and Tony's absolute need to be in walking distance of a newspaper and a cup of coffee.

The house was scented with spice. My friend Cindy had left a casserole of cinnamon chicken and a dish of her tahini, which is the best tahini I have ever tasted, and I have tasted it in twenty countries. Nicki, who had relieved our neighbors on dog-sitting duty, had warmed everything up and laid an attractive table. It was the first meal in three days that either Bizu or I had wanted to eat.

The kitchen was full of gifts of food, flowers, cards of condolence. The dogs, Bear and Simba, greeted us with oblivious canine joy. Bizu sank his face into the fur of the big one, Bear, grateful for lumbering, uncomplicated Labrador love.

Nathaniel texted that his flight out of Dallas was delayed by a tornado. It would board too late to connect with the last flight to the island. He would need to spend the night in Boston and catch the puddle jumper in the morning.

So Bizu and I went up to bed. I stood at the door of my empty bedroom. It was hard to enter. This was how it would be now: empty, always. I had been sleeping alone while Tony was on tour, so I tried to tell myself that this was no different. Bear knew better. As soon as I turned out the light and rolled over onto my side, she jumped up on the bed. Instead of taking her usual place at my feet, she laid her long dense body against mine, her spine to my spine. It was as if she were saying, "You're not alone."

The next morning I steeled myself to listen to the many messages on our home phone voicemail. The earliest, time-stamped just after I'd left the house as I scrambled to get to the ferry: the transplant team at George Washington hospital, asking for consent to use Tony's organs.

This devastated me. Of course, I would have given consent. Tony would have wanted it without question. His driver's license, which he had on him when he collapsed, identified him as an organ donor.

Why had they even needed to ask me? What was the point of stating your wish on your driver's license if that wish would not be respected? Why hadn't the resident asked me, or even mentioned that I would get this call? Why had we wasted someone's chance for life, for health?

Later, when I could think clearly, I realized that they couldn't have recovered his vital organs. They would have been failing, would have failed, even before he reached the ER. Perhaps they might have recovered his corneas. Corneas that might have restored someone's sight. Instead, a sizzle of moisture, evaporated in a split second in the crematorium.

In a few days, when I was not so devasted and not so emotional, I called back that transplant team and berated them for their failed process. "We can send you a certificate that says he would have been an organ donor had circumstances allowed. Some people find that helpful."

"What I would find 'helpful,'" I said through gritted teeth, "is knowing that you will make changes to ensure this doesn't happen again."

There were, of course, many other voicemails. One, recorded just before we had arrived home, was from Kris, our literary agent. She had left a message to say that *Spying on the South* was going to be on the *New York Times* bestseller list. It was the list tracking sales in the week before Tony died, so it represented the fruits of his work on tour, that exhausting eight cities in seven days.

I called her back and asked her if she thought he'd had any idea this would happen. "I told him I was cautiously optimistic," Kris said, "because some of his best events that first week were at stores that report to the *Times*. But I don't know if he really believed me."

I told Bizu about the bestseller list and emailed the news to Nathaniel, waiting in Boston to catch his flight to the Vineyard. He emailed me back: "And here he was worried not many people would read it. He would have been thrilled. Oh Dad."

For my part, I hardly knew how I felt. Of course I wanted his last work to be appreciated, to be beloved. But I still can't look at copies of *Spying on the South* without thinking, *There's the book that killed Tony*. The relentless effort of reporting it, the drug- and booze-enabled writing process, and finally the exhausting tour.

But how could it have been otherwise? Tony had always been that way. All in.

When I came to New York in September 1982 and began to make friends with my fellow graduate students at Columbia Journalism School, I quickly grasped the clear class and cultural differences between us. These people were driven in a way I never had been, and many of them seemed burned out even before they'd started their careers. They were weary, these twentysomethings. Many of them were veterans of the fight to get into the exclusive preschool, the prestige elementary, the elite prep. At every step, more pressure: arm yourself with perfect grades, load up extracurricular accomplishments. Acceptance to an elite graduate program at an Ivy League university was just another skirmish in their lifelong campaign.

My experience had been so different. "You arrived at the J-School as if you were coming to a ball," one friend observed years later. "I was astonished—you actually expected to enjoy it."

I did. I was grateful for the scholarship that had provided the opportunity to have a New York adventure and hone my reporting skills. My ambitions, such as they were, had always been my own. My parents had never pushed me. Whatever I did was just fine by them. If I got distinctions, they were thrilled, but they didn't expect them, and there was no sense that I'd disappoint them if I fell short. Both were from tough, unprosperous backgrounds and both had experienced some unlikely early success—my California-born dad as a singer, my Australian mum as a radio presenter. But for reasons I've never understood, long before I was born, they'd renounced those glamorous jobs and with them, seemingly, all ambition. They'd settled into a frugal life in a blue-collar neighborhood of Sydney. Mum became a housewife, Dad a proofreader. Our furniture was mostly secondhand, there was no car, we never traveled.

Tony, by contrast, came from a tribe of affluent high achievers, art on the walls, trips abroad, the best schools and colleges. It was a warm family, full of love, loud conversations, laughter, but also high expectations. It was understood that you must aspire to excellence, work hard, never stop striving.

When Tony and I teamed up on a story, as we often did on reporting assignments in the Middle East, I would occasionally have the temerity to suggest we might take some time off after grueling days and nights of reporting, maybe take a nap or a dip in the hotel pool before we launched into the writing. I might as well have suggested we throw ourselves off the balcony. Tony simply didn't function at less than 100 percent effort. It wasn't in his nature.

He had known for a very long time that this behavior might have consequences. In 1983, the year he started his first journalism job at the Fort Wayne *News-Sentinel*, he went to visit a fortune-teller. "You have the shortest lifeline I've ever seen," she reported. Later, he had a "scary revelation" while reading an article about type A personalities who suffer from "hurry sickness" and die young of heart attacks. He wrote in his journal: "I must rein in my anxieties. And again, vistas open of travel and exploration with g. and we must find the time somehow and not get caught up in CAREER."

Unfortunately, he did not hold that thought for long. Within a page or two of that same journal, he was fretting about his job prospects and planning his next move. He never managed to shed the hurry sickness, the driven temperament. Even when we decided to start a family, ten years into our marriage, he barely broke stride.

Although he tried. Anticipating how our life would change after Nathaniel was born, he left *The Wall Street Journal* and became a staff writer at *The New Yorker*, thinking that a magazine would offer more flexibility than being a national reporter for a daily paper.

It turned out to be a poor fit. He left an organization that had trusted his judgment for one that constantly second-guessed him. Last-minute late-night calls from a phalanx of editors only worsened the inevitable insomnia of new parenthood. Though he wrote some memorable pieces, he grew weary of superiors who wanted to know exactly what the story would say before he had even reported it, and then henpecked his writing into the early hours on the eve of every publication.

Luckily his third book, *Confederates in the Attic*, was a success. He signed a contract to write *Blue Latitudes*, about Captain Cook, and we decamped to Sydney and a less stressful life as full-time book writers. As he dove into the Cook archives, I started writing my first novel, and Nathaniel picked up an Australian accent that stuck with him for years. It was our second long stint living together in Sydney. We were more settled in our marriage, more confident in our work, and I recall it as a golden time. So many good memories: walking Nathaniel to his first day of kindergarten at a historic gum-tree-shaded schoolhouse where the kids' uniforms included wide-brimmed cloth hats to protect them from the powerful Aussie sun; afternoons watching him and his little mates clamber over the sandstone outcrops and dangle from trees in the remnant of foreshore bushland that had magically survived in our dense urban neighborhood. On the weekends the three of us would drive north and visit my mum at her house near the beach. She would overfeed us with roast dinners. After the meal, Tony, slayed, would bask on her backyard banana chair while Mum reveled in playtime with her grandson. It was an easier, less-pressured life than in the States. Our Aussie friends had a healthier work-life balance and while we lived there, we did, too.

But I couldn't keep Tony there. Even before *Blue Latitudes* was on the way to publication, the next thing, the next siren song, was calling him. So, while I know he would have been pleased and relieved that *Spying on the South* was a bestseller, it wouldn't have sated his need for the next accomplishment.

It was late morning by the time Bizu and I left to collect Nathaniel from the tiny airport, less than fifteen minutes from the house. Normally I'd have gone alone. But on this occasion, it seemed necessary that we both go. We didn't even discuss it. Bizu just got in the car.

This wobbly trio. It was how we would have to go on. We would have to learn to balance ourselves in an unfamiliar asymmetry.

And we would all have to learn to stop setting the table for four.

FLINDERS ISLAND

Bad dream last night.

Tony leaves me at home, watching a movie. He's going to pick up our friends, Jack and Lisa, and bring them back to the house. We're all going to watch the movie together. I'm enjoying the film, it's good. But after awhile I begin to wonder what's keeping them. Later I learn that Tony has met up with Jack and Lisa, and Bruce, our friend from Nashville, has joined them. They've all gone out and had a great night without me.

I am furious, but Tony is unrepentant. He doesn't respond to my hurt feelings. I know I can't let go of my anger until he says he is sorry, until he understands why it was wrong, until he makes it up to me in some act of atonement. But he shrugs it off. I don't understand his intransigence. I become angrier. I say horrible things.

The fury I feel toward him is so intense it wakes me up.

Throughout the day the dream hangs around me like a dank mist. Where has this come from, these cruel thoughts, those hateful words? I am as spent as if the dream argument were real.

Something is surfacing here. I don't yet see what it is. I walk the beach, head down against the wind. The salt air does not scour the bitterness from my spirit.

Tony has left me. He's gone on without me. That part is clear enough. But I am the one who still mingles with our old friends, who has the nights out, who still savors the precious experiences of the living. He is the one excluded. He is the one missing out.

So why am I angry at him? Not merely angry but enraged to an intensity I never felt toward him, even in our worst arguments.

That night I have trouble falling asleep. I fear more disturbing dreams. I am drifting, and then suddenly wide-awake. I can see it now.

Denial, then anger, says Kübler-Ross.

I am not angry with Tony.

I am furious with death.

WEST TISBURY

All the clocks do not stop. No one silences the phone. The dogs continue to bark, the pianos to play.

Old poet Wystan could not command the world to acknowledge his great loss. Neither can I. As much as I yearned to throw a black veil over my head and sit weeping under a yew tree, that was not possible.

Modern life is a juggling act, and if you don't keep those flaming torches moving swiftly through the air—if you lose your focus and drop one—the whole stage might catch fire and collapse beneath you.

As soon as the death certificate was signed, Tony's Social Security number triggered a cascade of consequences. My credit cards froze, because Tony was the primary cardholder. In my gray mist of sadness, I did not want to think about credit cards, but I had to, since our bills were paid that way, and if I didn't immediately get to work on making other arrangements, we mightn't have lights or phones the following month. I knew I was lucky to have the wherewithal to pay those bills. For so many the death of a spouse is also the death of the breadwinner. I was not going to be cast into penury and I was immensely grateful for that. But it didn't stop me from being enraged when my applications for new credit cards in my own name were rejected. I hadn't had an independent credit history since 1984. I had to start all over again. The one card I did eventually qualify for had a credit limit a tenth of the canceled ones.

In thirty-five years Tony and I had settled into an amicable division of labor within the marriage, taking responsibility for the tasks for which each of us had aptitude. I handled the things you could see—home maintenance, the garden, the cooking. He handled everything you couldn't see: finances, taxes, insurance. And he did it so skillfully that I had had the luxury of not ever having to consider those things at all.

Before he embarked on the Olmsted project, Tony had briefly considered writing a short book called *October Eggs*, a lighthearted look at finance. He didn't pursue it; he found his taboos around talking about money too strong. But he got as far as drafting a proposal. It started like this:

> *Here's the sad truth. I don't garden, or golf, or play the piano, or tinker in my toolshed. Instead, when I need respite, I buy and sell stocks, junk bonds, cotton futures, emerging market debt. As a boy I collected coins and slotted them into cardboard folders. As an adult I move assets in and out of my online portfolio. It's as close as I have to a hobby.*

*Managing money is also my rare contribution to the house-
hold. I'm a bad cook and worse handyman who kicks appliances
when they stop working. As my sons are quick to remind me,
Mom is the one who gets out the wrench or toilet plunger. But
there's one realm where Dad seems apt. He pays the bills and
magically multiplies our savings.*

Tony learned to read stock hieroglyphs at the knee of his grandfather,
a New Haven lawyer whose idea of a suitable outing for a visiting
grandchild was to take him to watch the ticker at Merrill Lynch.
From him Tony learned about investments, from the solidity of buy-
and-hold blue chips to the exciting riskiness of short selling and commodity futures. October Eggs was one of his grandfather's favorite
speculations.

This was all geek to me. My parents lived paycheck to paycheck, their
sole asset the modest house whose mortgage they worked hard to pay
off. I picked up a glancing acquaintance with price-earnings ratios and
yield curves in a brief stint covering business for *The Wall Street Journal*, but when I moved to the foreign desk, I happily forgot most of it
and was glad to let Tony take charge. In the car some afternoons, he'd
turn the satellite radio to a show in which noisy guys argued about
stocks. Tony thought one of them was astute and sometimes followed
his suggested trades. I hated the racket and begged him to switch the
station to *All Things Considered*. Now I wish I'd paid attention.

About once a year he would show me a pleasant page of mostly
green numbers that represented the performance of the investments he'd selected for our retirement accounts. But I never asked

him how he made those decisions. I wasn't even sure where those accounts were, or what passwords he used to access them, and when he died it was the last thing I wanted to be thinking about.

Or the second-to-last thing. Another flaming torch threatening to hit the floor was taxes. Tony got a filing extension every year and in early fall, when the deadline finally loomed, he would get a harried look and walk around the house muttering the name of our accountant under his breath, often preceded by expletives. We'd had the same accountant since the 1980s. He was a very strange man who kept vampire hours and refused to use email. You could only deal with him on the phone, and only late at night.

Here I will call him Baffert. Over the years, he had become increasingly eccentric. Tony began to catch errors. He had to double-check every filing, dreading a mistake that would lead to a long entanglement with the IRS.

Tony was an ardent list maker. I would find his to-do lists strewn about the house, scrawled on bits of cardboard or on the back of used envelopes, with emphatic, celebratory lines scratched through the accomplished tasks. One day I found a list that concluded with the item: *Check other list*.

When I got home, under a bag of gifted muffins on the kitchen counter, I found Tony's last list before he left on book tour. On it were things he meant to do as soon as he returned. The first item:

Fire Baffert.

Flinders Island

I have had to change shacks. Mick, the farmer, needed his place for visiting family, so I have packed up my things and moved a few miles south to a different stretch of the western coastline. On the map, it doesn't look far, but as soon as I turn off the main road, a rough track winds and twists interminably through dense bushland. My tied-together-with-twine vehicle creaks and squeals with resentment. It's difficult going and I'm relieved when the gate to the new place finally appears between stands of feathery casuarinas.

This new shack is a bit smaller and a little fancier: it has the bathroom indoors and a rather chic kitchen. It's also even more remote. It makes Killiecrankie's sparse scatter of cottages feel like a metropolis. In a recent census, its location, Leeka, registered a population of nil.

When I've described the place to friends, some have asked me if I was afraid to be alone in such an isolated spot. The truth is that it never even occurred to me to be anxious. It's not as if I'm a fearless person. I am a nervous passenger in fast cars; I'm also scared to go far from shore when swimming in rough surf. But I am never worried about being alone—not in the city and certainly not in the bush. I put it on the same shelf of unlikely risks as being struck by lightning or swallowed by quicksand.

The shack sits right above a small beach. Another glorious view. A long arm of rocky reef slings itself from the north to create a sheltered bay. A low swell of cave-pocked granite defines the southern end. The shack looks northwest across a wide expanse of open sea. A single small island, low on the horizon, is all that stands between me and the southern Indian Ocean. To the east, past the granite outcrop, the wide, white sands of Marshall Bay extend in a slow curve all the way to Wybalenna and Settlement Point in the far distance. In all that distance there is no other dwelling to be seen. The property is 140 acres of casuarina, grass trees, sedges, ribbon gums, and Tasmanian blue gums, interrupted by sculpted boulders.

The most remarkable of these rises abruptly, massive, taller than a four-story building. One face is a sheer vertical cliff, perfectly smooth as if sheared on a plumb line by a master stonemason. The other side is a rising cluster of curves. There is a shallow cave at the point where the two sides, the yin and yang of these hard and soft geometries, touch each other. The pink stone merges at the apex in a form that suggests a Gothic three-pointed arch, or a pair of hands coming together in prayer.

It feels like a sacred site, most definitely one dedicated to Mother Earth. For both sides of the looming declivity are gently rounded, like labial folds, sheltering the mystery within. I feel called to do something ceremonial in this place: to praise the beauty of Gaia, to atone for our crimes against her creation, to make a mother's prayer for safe keeping of my sons.

There is no sound but the waves and the gentle susurrus of the casuarinas. And as dark falls, the wind drops, and the white caps subside, not even that.

I settle into the solitude.

WEST TISBURY

All I craved was to be alone with the boys. But that would not be possible. Too many neighbors and friends wanted to express their sadness and could not wait till memorials that we had decided would happen in August on the Vineyard and October in DC. If we didn't see these kind friends jointly, we would have to deal with them severally. I would not be able to go to the supermarket without being run over by people expressing their sorrow in the vegetable aisle.

There would have to be a gathering, a sort-of *shiva*. We decided on Sunday evening.

But first I needed to get through Saturday, which was the day Tony would have been coming home from book tour. He would have been so happy; relieved to be done with travel, pleased to know he'd made the bestseller list, glad to have Bizu home from school for the summer, looking forward to Nathaniel's return from his wanderings. We would have had so much to celebrate.

Instead, between worrying about where everyone would park the next day and ordering sides of smoked salmon, I gave myself permission to get quietly, miserably hammered.

Sunday afternoon was cool and foggy. We dragged all the chairs out into the garden to form a wide circle under the boughs of the old apple tree. My posse of women friends gathered early and formed a flying wedge around me, managing the flow of people and cars and plates and glasses. They are generally a rowdy lot, these writers, teachers, artists, filmmakers. It was odd to see them subdued by sadness, speaking in hushed voices, tripping over one another in my kitchen, so anxious to be helpful.

There was a strangeness to the event. A discordant vibration. So many joyful summer gatherings had occurred on this lawn. Two weddings, numerous book parties, parties for no reason other than Tony's love of a party. As the crowd gathered, I kept catching almost-glimpses of him in a turn of a shoulder, the glint of late-afternoon sunlight on blond hair. I noticed Nathaniel, wrung out with jet lag, leaning for support on his girlfriend. I noticed Bizu as he greeted friends with a gracious dignity, his comportment suddenly adult. I noticed his eyes on me, anxious to see if I was doing okay, knowing I dreaded this as much as he did.

I had discovered I could best manage my own grief if I wasn't confronted with the tears of others. Some friends took my cue, some did not. What saved me was the unexpected arrival from Boston of Ron, the third in the trio of Tony's Columbia Journalism School roommates and later a colleague at *The Wall Street Journal*. Ron has a big personality like Tony's; like Tony, he is a natural emcee at any gathering. He became my buttress and a welcome leavening amid all the sadness.

Our rabbi began a service with readings from the Psalms. Then she said: "These are ancient texts that assume a God who controlled everything, and Tony would have a problem with that. So here are some modern psalms. . . ." She had chosen poems that were apt and personal to Tony. I remember especially these lines from Mary Oliver:

> *Pay attention.*
> *Be astonished.*
> *Tell about it.*

And this one, also:

> Doesn't everything die at last, and too soon?

After that reading, we stood under the apple boughs and said *kaddish*.

FLINDERS ISLAND

Social, monogamous, partial migrant, semiaquatic, congregatory.

These adjectives might have described Tony. In fact, they are the attributes of the Cape Barren goose, *Cereopsis novaehollandiae*, as listed in *Animalia*. They are one of the rarest of the world's geese, but they nest in large numbers on Flinders Island, making their home in its temperate wetlands and the tussock grasses around the shack.

Encountering them is a high point of my walks. They are amusing birds, bulky and inelegant, pale gray with pink legs and a vivid green cere atop their beak, which somehow gives them a quizzical expression. Their call is unmelodic, more like the grunt of a pig than any birdsong.

The *Australian Journal of Zoology* describes the bird somewhat unscientifically as "a most peculiar goose of uncertain affiliations," meaning, as far as I can gather, that ornithologists haven't decided if it is more like a swan or more like a duck. For a long time scientists mistakenly believed Cape Barren geese were the immature phase of the black swan. By the 1950s they'd been almost hunted to extinction. Easy-to-catch birds like these—the great auk, the moa, the heath hen—have not fared well at human hands. But just in time for the Cape Barren geese, the establishment of nature reserves such as those on Flinders allowed the population to gradually rebound.

These geese travel in large groups that have been given evocative names: gaggle, plump, skein, wedge, team. In my solitude I appreciate their sociability.

Tony was always much better in a gaggle than I. Though I managed to overcome my shyness by the time I finished my degree at Sydney Uni, I was never—will never be—the extrovert he was. I hid behind his outgoing social nature, clinging to him limpet-like at parties. When we had people over, I enjoyed making the food while he carried the conversation; a warmhearted, enthusiastic host.

He could never have settled on a place as small as Flinders Island. His personality demanded a larger canvas. Martha's Vineyard had worked for him because its influx of summer residents was so large and diverse, swelling our small year-round pod of friends with others from across the world. Tony made connections easily; his genuine curiosity, his willingness to ask the unguarded question, to sometimes go out on precarious conversational limbs, disarmed people used to cautious deference. The longer we lived on the island, the wider the circle of friends became, until summer's social obligations sometimes seemed overwhelming. My more introverted nature occasionally yearned for the days when we'd known no one and spent our island time beachcombing or rambling in the woods.

In the summers since Tony died, I have found myself straining to retain the level of sociability of our old life together. The Cape Barren geese in their gaggles remind me how much I miss Tony's talent for hosting. Remembering how I used to enjoy feeding a big mob of people around my table, I have tried to continue.

But without him, the gaggles will never be the same.

WEST TISBURY

Our family attorney, George, is a neighbor. He knows more than anyone should know about loss and had sent a heartfelt condolence message.

On the Monday morning after the *shiva*, Nathaniel and I drove the short distance to his office to learn what we must do next in this obstacle course of legally ending a life.

George had drawn up new wills for Tony and me in 2008, right after we returned home from Ethiopia with Bizu. Eleven years later, Nathaniel and I sat down at his polished conference table and paged through the thick document. It was much more complicated than I remembered.

When we got married Tony and I had made simple wills. We didn't have much of anything then and we wrote up one-page documents, each leaving our mite to the other. After we'd bought a house, had Nathaniel, adopted Bizu, it had seemed prudent to update these.

I hadn't focused on that task. I was still working through the blizzard of paperwork around Bizu's adoption. We had legally adopted him according to Ethiopian law, but once we brought him home we needed to do it all again under US law at Dukes County courthouse. I was burnt out on legalese and far more fixated on getting a wary child settled into our family than reviewing wills. Conversations between Tony and George—about possible changes to estate tax laws, Massachusetts rules and federal rules, marital trusts and remainder trusts—went sailing right over my head. Taxes, trusts: these were in Tony's wheelhouse. While I did read through the thirty or so pages of my revised will, which was the mirror image of Tony's, it did not sink in that what we were creating was a convoluted edifice, unwarranted by the size of our assets or our simple wishes.

Now I was about to pay for my inattention.

This fancy document was more complicated than the usual run of year-round Vineyarders' wills. The clerk at the local probate court was new in the job and cautious. Nervous about the will's implications, she had advised the judge that it could not be probated until a guardian *ad litem* was appointed to protect the interests of Bizu, a minor.

I had never heard of guardians *ad litem*. A quick internet search revealed that these are appointed in situations of contested wills, family dysfunction, acrimonious divorces, gross incompetence.

None of this applied to us. I was stunned that the court sought to violate my rights as a parent in this way. How could they suggest that I, Bizu's mother, could not be trusted to have his best interests at heart? The assets in the will were assets that Tony and I had amassed together. To have some court-appointed stranger supervising my agency over their disposition was galling. I couldn't imagine the law treating a competent surviving father in this way.

I told George that I would not consent to this, that I would fight it in court. It was another thing I did not want to be thinking about, another interruption to the business of grieving. I felt I had no choice.

I no longer recognized my desk. We'd bought the narrow walnut tavern table when we moved from Cairo to London, to a tiny eighteenth-century terrace house in Hampstead. It had been our dining table, even though the Gulf War and other crises we'd been constantly called away to cover hadn't allowed for a lot of domesticity. Those were the years when our duffel bags stood half-packed in the closet, filled with accoutrements of foreign correspondence— shortwave radios, field dressings, bricks of cash for countries that didn't take cards, my chador, a bulletproof vest. Later, when our lives changed and we had time for dinner parties, the small tavern table moved upstairs to my office, and a library table that seated twenty took its place in the dining room.

I was used to seeing my desk covered with notes for my fiction, not legal documents, financial spreadsheets, and baskets of condolence notes. For a week or so, I individually answered each one of these notes. By the second week, there were hundreds. I resorted to photocopying a heartfelt thank-you note and hired a friend's daughter to address envelopes for the replies. I valued these letters, especially the ones that recounted an anecdote about Tony that I hadn't known. I was also overwhelmed by them. As they kept coming, and coming, I felt reproached by the stack, rising unanswered on my desk as I dealt instead with each legal and financial exigency. I hoped friends would forgive my failure, finally, to respond to them. I would drag myself into my study to face the latest pile of documents and wonder if I would ever do anything creative again.

Just as the paperwork threatened to bury me, my sister arrived from Australia. We had spent our adult lives propping each other up through difficult times. After my mother's health began to fail and she came to live with me, Darleen traveled often to the Vineyard, to stand shoulder-to-shoulder with me as we managed her various medical emergencies. Now she hauled me away from my desk, from the enraging legal documents, the baffling numbers. She made decent Australian tea—hot and strong. We walked the beaches, breathing the warming late-spring air. With her beside me, I felt able to venture out on everyday errands, where islanders— taciturn New Englanders—expressed their condolences with wordless hugs or packages of fresh fish for which they would accept no payment.

However, there were binding decisions to be made, even if I was in a poor condition to make them. I needed to gather affidavits for the motion to waive the guardian appointment, mortified by asking people to testify to my ability to care for my child. After all the paperwork was filed, I waited for a court date in front of the busy traveling judge who came to the island only twice a month. When our matter at last made its way onto his docket, my attorney and I trekked to the Edgartown courthouse, past sunlit clapboard houses, their picket fences tousled with roses and hydrangeas in full bloom. In the gloomy courtroom we sat through case after miserable case about family tragedy, feuding, and dysfunction until, finally, it was my chance to be heard.

Having to stand up in court and defend my right to mother my own son was, I thought, the final cruelty in this cruel bureaucracy of death.

But I was wrong about that.

FLINDERS ISLAND

Porphyritic granite. Coarse gravels. Silica-rich soils. Folded sedimentary sequences. Scattered, scoured, angular blocks of siltstone, honeycombed by wind and sea. Large K-feldspar phenocrysts. Basalt xenoliths. The Blue Tier batholith, Upper Devonian period.

There is nothing like a geological timeline to put you in your place.

When the seas rose between twelve and eighteen thousand years ago, they left Flinders and the other Bass Strait islands as all that remains of the land bridge that once linked the Australian mainland to Tasmania. Eighteen thousand years is not that long ago in human generations. If you figure there are four generations every century, forty every thousand years, about seven hundred generations have lived and died since this island became an island. I try to imagine each generational death: who was mourned, who was the mourner. When early death was ubiquitous, was the pain of loss any less, or did the precarity of life make each loss even more painful?

These are the questions raised by the rocks. A third of this island is rugged granite mountain range. I had not known this common rock could be so various, so beautiful. I imagine the seething earth that gave rise to these rocks; the searing heat, the molten ores, the cracking and hissing as solid earth forced through liquid ocean, the acrid fumes, the scalding ash. Chaos and cacophony slowly subsiding into solidity, into silence.

The shack has some books on the natural history of the island, and I devour the chapters on its geology, rappelling into caverns of unfamiliar vocabulary.

Batholith, from the Greek for "depth" and "stone," was coined by the Germans in the early twentieth century and imported into English, that promiscuous word-borrower, soon after. Phenocryst, also from the Greek: *phaneros*, "conspicuous, shining"; *kristallos*, "gem." Phenocrysts are show-offs, five times bigger than surrounding crystals in the rock. I wonder if diamonds are phenocrysts. When I look it up, I learn that the answer is no. They are xenocrysts— foreign gems—carried up from the earth's mantle, torn off the sides of the magma pipes surging up through the crust.

When Tony and I married, I wore a diamond ring that had belonged to his great-grandmother, Bubbe Rose. There hadn't been an engagement ring. I did not want one, any more than I wanted the other expensive trappings of the wedding-industrial complex. I bought an inexpensive off-the-rack outfit—a white angora sweater over a lacy slip dress. My sister and I did all the cooking at her home on a hillside in France. To satisfy secular French law, we were married by the mayor in the sixteenth-century village town hall, and then a rabbi wed us again, in my sister's garden, among the lavender and the broom, with just fifteen people in attendance. The *chuppah* was a tallit strung on pieces of doweling we bought the day before at the local *bricolage*. I'd forgotten to pack nice shoes so those, too, were bought last-minute and pinched my toes all day.

But I was glad to wear that fancy diamond ring in its antique platinum setting. Tony's mother, Ellie, gave it to me, just before the wedding. It signified my acceptance into a lineage of women who had endured, survived, and prospered against huge odds: survivors of pogrom and exile, immigrants, matriarchs.

At the wedding feast Ellie read a poem she had composed. A prolific writer of books for children and young adults, Ellie was famed for her witty "occasional poems" at family gatherings, and this one highlighted the unlikeliness of our union:

> *If in Sydney you start to dig*
> *Into the earth at a steady pace*
> *A trillion zillion miles away*
> *You'll come up in Chevy Chase.*
>
> *If in Maryland you begin*
> *To search the world both far and near*

> *Once you've covered terra cognita*
> *You'll find there's a whole other hemisphere!*

As Ellie pointed out, the odds of our meeting had been ridiculously long. It had happened on a balcony in Manhattan, at a party thrown by a classmate the first week of graduate school. Tony was a tanned, tousle-haired blond in overalls and red sneakers, regaling the small group on the balcony with the woes of living with his brother in Alphabet City, which in those years was a rough corner of the Lower East Side. He'd learned that the local crooks had a small scam: steal the battery from your car, then sell it back to you from the neighborhood vendor of used auto parts. He'd bought his battery back twice before he realized he had to take the car key *and* the battery with him when he parked.

The next day, when the class gathered in Columbia's World Room for our official welcome from the dean, I saw the amusing blond across the room. I waved. He did not wave back. I thought, *That's rude*, and didn't think of him again for the rest of the semester.

After winter break we learned we'd both signed up, on a whim, for the class on business reporting. Each of us had reasoned that we needed some tools to understand capitalism if we aspired to report on its failures and excesses.

In class I was attracted to his idealism (and to be honest, his sculpted forearms). He'd come to journalism school from Meridian, Mississippi, where he'd been working as a union organizer, trying to get fair pay for poor Black woodcutters. Over spring break he'd been back there with Josh, making a documentary, *Mississippi Wood*, that would eventually air on PBS. With his shirtsleeves pushed up, I noted his arms were attractively tanned a rich hazelnut. For my part, I was pallid as a bedsheet, having spent the spring break on a trip for young journalists to the Soviet Union.

As we got to know each other, I learned that he hadn't waved back to me that morning in the World Room because he had been out celebrating with his brother the night before, had lost his glasses down the toilet at Danceteria and couldn't even see me. Later he'd been dissuaded from seeking me out because he noticed that at seminars, I always sat with a handsome classmate named Bronstein, and he assumed we were an item. I had to point out to him that seating for that seminar was alphabetical by surname.

We got seriously involved the last week of classes, our first kiss beneath the unlovely footbridge over Amsterdam Avenue. This was suboptimal timing for a new relationship, since I had already accepted a job in *The Wall Street Journal*'s Cleveland bureau, and he was heading to an internship on the West Coast. It seemed our affair would be a brief grad school fling and nothing more.

But on his drive west, he stopped to see me in Cleveland over the weekend. I was apartment hunting and the *Journal* had put me up in a downtown hotel. On Monday, after Tony had left, I returned from work to find the bland décor of my hotel room brightened by a hand-pieced quilt, made of sugar bags and work shirts that Tony had acquired in Mississippi. Meanwhile, as Tony drove west, the radio in his car died, just a few miles out of Cleveland. He had the entire trip across the country with nothing to do but think about the wonderful time we'd just had. A few weeks later he turned around and came back. He found employment as education reporter on the Fort Wayne *News-Sentinel*—a four-hour drive from Cleveland and the closest reporting job he could get. On Friday nights we took turns driving through blizzards to spend our days off together. A year and a half later, we were married at my sister's house in the Alpes-Maritimes, and Tony's mother read her poem about how this unlikely love affair had beaten the odds.

WEST TISBURY

Tony, the historian, loved graveyards. As a kid, he had made rubbings of the bleak old Puritan death's heads that decorate so many New England tombstones. Yet he would have no stone, no marker, no mausoleum.

He had always resisted talking about death.

Having cared for my mother through the prolonged thievery of Alzheimer's disease, I was a proponent of advance directives, strident about the kind of end-of-life experience I did not want. Tony refused to take part in these conversations. He would find an urgent errand that he absolutely had to get done that very minute and hurry from the room. He didn't want to think about our old age or the possibility of his own future infirmity. And as it turned out, he didn't have to.

The one thing he had stated was that he wanted his ashes to be buried in his baseball mitt in the unkempt Chilmark field where he played softball on summer Sunday mornings. This may have been a flippant remark, but the boys and I decided that since they were the only instructions we had, we would carry them out.

He loved that softball game and the odd array of island characters who showed up for it. Every Sunday he would bring me coffee and *The New York Times*, then rush off to be there for "mitts in," the ritual where players threw their gloves into a pile and the league's "commissioners" took turns picking them up, filling team rosters at random. It was a game with a long tradition and its own lighthearted rules. A ball hit as far as the dirt track at the edge of the field was known as a Kerouac, because it was on the road. A ball that landed in the poison ivy patch counted as a homer, since no one was expected to plunge in to catch it. When Bizu was eight and playing Little League, he accompanied Tony to the games and served as pinch runner for some of the arthritic older players. When at season's end he was named Rookie of the Year, Tony was delighted.

After every game Tony would sit at the kitchen table cackling to himself as he wrote outlandish "after-action reports" full of scurrilous fabrications about the morning's play. When one player, Jerry, had a knee replacement, Tony inflated the procedure into a fictious series of operations that had resulted in Jerry becoming entirely bionic. He took to referring to him with inverted commas.

"Labor Day is always bittersweet at Flanders Field and was especially so this year due to the tragic quality of the play," he wrote in a typical dispatch to his teammates. "Among the bonehead moves: a rare mental error by 'Jerry,' steaming towards third, which was already occupied by a teammate. 'That's why I'm having my next surgery tomorrow,' he said, after being tagged out. 'Artificial intelligence.'"

Another player, known for his ardent support of the Israeli right, also came in for constant mockery. "Joel G. lifted his shirt to show off his rippling Ai-pac from hard workouts with the Judea and Samaria League. He then flashed some fine leather and trash talk, applying a Philadelphia tag to my solar plexus so hard that I lost my breath. 'Take that, you running-dog, raghead-loving J-Streeter!' he gleefully shouted." The teammates enjoyed the ribbing and created a special Fake News Award for Tony, complete with its own trophy.

His ashes arrived in a beautiful handmade paper container embossed with pressed ferns and wildflower seeds, ready for an eco-burial.

I found his lefty mitt in the box where we kept sporting gear. I pressed it to my face, smelling the leather and sweat, thinking of the joy on his face as he ran backward, squinting into the sun, reaching for a long fly ball. I picked a bunch of native columbines, and we headed to the field to fulfill his wishes.

It's a scruffy field down a dirt road opposite the Chilmark town dump. But it is surrounded by woods, and on a breezy day the branches fan the air with a peaceful whisper. I dug out a neat square of sod and then let the boys take over to dig the hole, trying not to make too much disturbance to the field ahead of summer's

Opening Day. When we replaced the sod, I put the flowers on top. We stood beside this eccentric grave, hugging, weeping. It was Father's Day.

That night the wind would blow the flowers away, and by the following summer it would be impossible to discern where we'd dug. His memorial would exist only in the memories of laughter and good times on those Sunday mornings when he had been happy.

Later my sister wrote a poem that included these lines:

> *There he rests in a cradle of a hand*
> *Cushioned in familiar folds of skin that he once held*
> *Together they leapt into the light*
> *Catching and returning with speed*
> *Caps off as you pass that field*
> *It holds treasure in it.*

FLINDERS ISLAND

There is a dead bird on the deck in front of the shack. It lies perfect, unbloodied, a fragment of prey still clenched firmly in its beak.

It must have collided with the glass of the sliding door. Humans; always lethally in the way of other species.

The death is recent. The bird's round eye is darkly luminous. Ants have not found it yet. I gather up the tiny corpse. It fits into the palm of my hand. The feathers are a warm russet on the back and wings, the breast patterned in scallops of white and tan. There is a long, jaunty tail. It's not a bird I know, and there are no birding books in the shack. Later, when I am able to get a field guide, the closest match I find is the brown thornbill.

I carry it out to the trees and place it carefully on a soft bed of fallen casuarina fronds. The morsel tenaciously trapped in its beak appears to be a spider leg. This late in the summer, it is unlikely the bird was bringing the arachnid to nestlings. I hope it enjoyed its last meal before that sudden ending.

The following morning, as I walk down to the beach, movement catches my eye. The bird is fluttering. For a second logic fails me and I think that it was only stunned and now is recovering. But as I move closer, I see that the vitality does not belong to the bird. It is the frenzied motion of maggots, feasting. The thornbill writhes and twitches, all a-ripple with the undulations of countless worms concealed beneath its feathers. They are efficient, this ravenous horde. A day later there is little left. A fleshless tangle of feathers, a scatter of stripped bones.

It should be a repulsive image, yet I find it consoling: this bird, who met its unforeseen ending with a meal half-consumed, now devoured in a riotous jitterbug.

May my own death be just as sudden. Spare me the crematorium. Put me straight into the soil. I want to be part of this dance.

WEST TISBURY

---

*F*ire *Baffert.*

So said Tony's to-do list for after his book tour, above a succession of more easily actionable items, like *Pick Up Mower* and *Julia Graduation Gift.*

Fire Baffert. I stared at his handwriting. It was an unequivocal instruction. But, how? Tony could have fired our accountant of thirty years, I can't. I don't know enough. The last time I filled out a tax return, I was a newbie reporter at *The Wall Street Journal'*s Cleveland bureau, and the company withheld my taxes. I don't have a clue how it has worked for the decades we've been self-employed. I don't know about estimated taxes; I didn't know I'd already missed the June installment until I got slapped with a penalty. Baffert hadn't thought to mention it to me when I'd called him to ask about things I might need to do.

Still, I didn't fire Baffert.

I hired an accountant to manage my accountant. I handed her all the folders of receipts and statements I had found in Tony's study so she could sort it into an order Baffert could work with. And if he made a mistake, she was tasked with catching it.

I also hired a financial adviser. He looked over the edifice of investments that Tony had chosen to secure our future, frowned at the crypto, squinted at the China stocks ("China's too opaque"), and recommended I divest those positions and buy bonds instead. I could almost hear Tony yawning at the thought of low-risk munis and boring AAAs.

"As long as you can keep writing and don't conceive a sudden desire to buy a private jet, I think you're going to be okay," the adviser declared.

Keep writing. There was the catch. There would be no paycheck for me until I handed in a finished manuscript of *Horse*.

I didn't see how I would ever get it finished. I was only about half-way into the story and hadn't added a word since Tony had died. Hadn't even opened the file on my computer since the day I'd picked up the phone and learned that he was gone. It was not a do-able thing.

Writing fiction requires a wombat-hole immersion. You go down into that dark, narrow place where there is nothing else but you and the unspooling story. There was no space down there for court motions and tax filings, for memorial planning and condolence-note replies.

And there was certainly no place for the beast of grief clinging to me, claws intractable as fishhooks.

FLINDERS ISLAND

For years, until he started full-time book writing, Tony had kept a journal. Some years in nice leatherbound diaries, some years in ratty spiral notebooks. These were his private thoughts and, apart from one explosive incident early in our courtship, I had never violated that privacy.

Now I will read them. Columbia University wants his papers. An archivist has already been to the house and sorted them into boxes, ready for transport to Butler Library.

My sister, who is a biographer, has counseled me to go through everything before I send it away. Several times, sitting in archives, she had found herself confronted by profoundly intimate revelations that she felt were not intended for a stranger's gaze. Tony loved deep diving in archives, but I'm not certain how he would feel about every musing contained in these numerous boxes. I am inclined to believe that he would prefer his papers to leave here uncensored, whatever they might reveal. But I do want some private time with his thoughts before I ship them away.

I have brought four of his journals with me, pulled at random from one of the boxes. I sit on the deck and begin to revisit our lives.

By chance I have pulled out the journal from the year we met, the year at Columbia, so I start there. I quickly see my sister's point about "intimate revelations." He had arrived at Columbia in the process of slowly, miserably extricating himself from a passionate but doomed undergraduate affair. In the fall semester, part of getting over it apparently entailed sleeping with a fair number of our Columbia classmates.

I giggle with amazement as the list lengthens: Her, as well? Not *her*, of all people?

Then I come to the entry for December 31, 1982. We are halfway through journalism school at that point, and he and I have not yet started taking the business reporting class together. He makes a New Year's resolution to view his writing "NOT as a mood activity, but as work to be done each and every day. So, yes, you may write better on a stoned Saturday night, but it is the weekday mornings of throwaways that make those moments of inspiration fluid, and it has been a long time since my writing felt fluid in that manner, and sometime this spring I will recapture it, my talent will come clear,

I hope. what else, what else for the new year. 1983. A meaningless number, no resonance whatsoever. nothing. let it come."

What comes, of course, is us. My first appearance in this narrative is at the end of March and inauspicious. It had been a bleak day for him: a day of ill health, long lines at the student medical center, and an altercation with one of his casual paramours, who tells him she hates him and throws a beer in his face.

Apparently we'd made a bet on something, and I'd won it, so he owed me a bottle of champagne. He writes: "get drunk on champagne with Geraldine and things are all right." I do not appear again till May, the very end of the school year, and once again as a consoling figure. He had hoped to win a traveling fellowship, but it had gone to someone else. "Geraldine turning to me tonight in the restaurant and saying 'I won't say any more about it after this but that was stupid. There is no justice in it.' and she is always so wise, but let it all go, and I will . . . and at the same time as all this some intimacy as not in recent memory, but is it just her intellect and cleverness and blue eyes?"

By the end of this journal, he has just moved to Fort Wayne to be near me, and our relationship is an established and serious thing. I want to follow our story in his telling but that will have to wait. I curse myself for not having brought consecutive journals. The next one I have begins in December 1985. It is our second year married. After our wedding we'd moved to Sydney. My father was dying of emphysema, and I wanted to be home to spend time with him and to support my mum. I'd hoped Tony would love Sydney and we would build a life there.

It looked promising. Even before his jet lag wore off, he was hired by *The Sydney Morning Herald*. In Fort Wayne, he'd managed to carve out a little space for enterprise writing, but he was required to cover school boards and do all the busywork of a beat reporter. The *Herald* quickly came to trust his instincts and let him choose his own stories, even outlandish ideas like hitchhiking across the Outback and sending back dispatches. It turned into a series full of humor and insights about the Australian character. Not long after the final installment, Tony received a letter:

> *Dear Mr Horwitz,*
>
> *For some time now I have been an admirer of your writing in the Sydney Morning Herald. Should you wish to pursue any particular topic in greater depth, i.e. a book, I would love the opportunity to discuss it with you.*

The writer was an editor at Harper and Row, and the book, *One for the Road: A Hitchhiker's Outback*, was published in Australia in 1987 and picked up in the United States the following year for Vintage Departures, Random House's celebrated travel imprint. Tony was thrilled by this, and as he dived into the project, he began to see that book writing, rather than daily journalism, might be his true calling. He didn't get much support for that notion when he broached it in a phone call with his dad. "We have twenty books in this family and nothing to show for it," his father opined. When Tony relayed that remark to me, it was with a laugh. Still, that pressure for conventional "success" kept him restless. In his journal on New Year's Eve 1986, he wrote: "It is perhaps telling that this morning I reached the last sentence of the book, and tonight I type out a letter to the Wash. Post—already, compulsively, on to the next thing."

The Washington Post, as it turned out, remained uninterested. ("We're top heavy with white Jewish males," one editor confided. "You represent a risk compared to applicants we've been following for some years," reflected another. And from *Newsday*: "You wouldn't want this job. Even if you got it. Which I don't think you will.")

So Tony threw himself into his *Herald* job, writing page-one stories and memorable features. Then, one night in early May 1987, just after dinner, as we were settling in on the couch with a video of *Three Days of the Condor*, the phone rang. "You don't have to answer it," Tony sighed. But I was worried about my dad's health. Thinking it might be a call from my mum, I hauled myself out from under his arm. It was *The Wall Street Journal*'s foreign editor. This was alarming. I had been working for her for two years, and she had never called. My latest story had been a piece about climate scientists in New Zealand studying the methane output of sheep. Was I about to get reprimanded for putting too many farting sheep jokes in *The Wall Street Journal*?

Tony had paused the video and gone to the bathroom. He came back to hear me saying, "Well, the Middle East would be great."

My *Journal* career until then (reporting basic industry in Cleveland; jaunting around Australia writing colorful pieces on Outback cattle drovers and barge captains hauling supplies to remote Aboriginal communities) hadn't exactly prepared me for a job of that scope. But Tony was intrigued by the high-risk/high-reward nature of the offer: I would be Mideast correspondent, based in Cairo, covering twenty-two countries. He would freelance for the paper on a regular basis with a staff position dangled as a possibility somewhere down the road. We played a mind game and found neither of us could name the leader of any Arab state, nor were we entirely certain of the latest prime minister in Israel. Was Sudan above or below Ethiopia? We had no right to take the job, knowing so little.

And yet we moved to Cairo, and made it work. Tony wrote for the *Journal*, but also for many others, including *The Dallas Morning News*, *The Courier-Journal* (Louisville), and for magazines such as *Harper's*. Within ten months of arriving, he'd banged out fifty-six stories for ten different publications. I had the prestige title and the steady paycheck, but he had the adventures. I was tied to the must-have-it stories of Arab summits and head-of-state interviews. While I sat in the gilded salons of ministerial offices being lied to, he went riding through the desert with the last Egyptian Camel Transport Corps or hitched a ride on a Goan dhow plying the mine-strewn waters of the Persian Gulf.

He scored a second book contract to write a Mideast memoir, *Baghdad without a Map*, in which he captured our bifurcated work lives. In Yemen, he wrote about being invited to chew qat in the mud-brick home of a traditional Sufi healer. As he reclined on pillows, getting high in a room with windows of stained glass and alabaster, "Mansour turned on the television news, without sound. The screen showed a Western woman standing with a pad and pen, interviewing Yemen's president. The image startled me. It looked just like Geraldine. Then I realized it *was* Geraldine, not a qat hallucination. I was glad to see she was getting on with her itinerary. Getting on with mine, I slumped deeper into the pillow and nibbled at a last green sprig of qat."

Two years after that Yemen trip, the longed-for staff job hadn't materialized. He was still a stringer and despondent about his prospects. Alone in Cairo on February 27, 1989, he wrote: "It seems very remote now that I shall ever really amount to something in journalism."

Reading this, alone on the deck, I hoot with laughter. By Christmas of that same year, he would be dodging rifle fire on the streets of Timişoara, covering Romania's revolution as the new star reporter in *The Wall Street Journal's* London bureau. Not long after we would both be back in the Middle East, leading the paper's coverage of the first Gulf War. Tony would scoop the competition as the first US reporter into Kuwait City with the liberating troops. We'd jointly win an Overseas Press Club Award for our coverage of the war. Then, four years later, he'd win the Pulitzer Prize for National Reporting, for a *Journal* series, "9 to Nowhere," on low-wage work in America.

By chance I have also packed his journal for the year he won the Pulitzer. In it I find a self-deprecating account of collecting the prize in New York, feeling "the establishment embrace" as he chats with luminaries of the old guard—Shelby Coffey, Seymour Topping, Fred Friendly—over "wine and salmon and a few words from Peter Kann, standard stuff about how this will follow us to the obituary page." Then, at the airport, the leaded crystal trophy embossed with Joseph Pulitzer's head sets off the metal detector. "I take it out of the bubble wrap and the security guard doesn't even bother glancing at it. Back to the real world, you schmuck, who cares about your damn prize!"

But he was happy at that lunch, handsome in the same wheat-colored linen suit he'd worn at our wedding (the reporting he did almost never required a suit, so it hadn't seen much wear), flanked by parents thrilled by his achievement.

So much for never amounting to something in journalism.

As funny as I find it, I'm also a bit sad to learn that he had battled such crushing insecurity. He hadn't disclosed how despondent he was. These journals, in general, are not happy reading. My sunny, funny lover is rarely found in these pages. I begin to see that he turned to his journals when he was *not* that guy—that guy didn't need them. "Happiness writes white," said the French author Henry de Montherlant; it is not easily inscribed on the page. Dark thoughts, fears, the insecure ramblings of insomniac nights—these are more easily prodded with the pen, the ink more easily spilled, more legible. So it comes as a relief and a joy when I also find this: "Our marriage still the one thing I feel is utterly mine, created out of clean cloth, no taint of all that makes me uncomfortable, my refuge.

Without her, god knows . . . really sure of nothing but her these days, of my love for her which I wish I knew better how to express."

And I wish I could tell him that he expressed it just fine.

I put the journals aside and go walking, marveling at how little we can know of our future, fretting that the Tony of 1989 had no sense how bright and successful his career was quickly about to become.

As I kick at the sand, the corollary occurs to me.

I'm thankful that the Tony of 2019 had no sense that his future was about to vanish abruptly, on a street corner, with a plummet into the dark. We know both things are possible—the glittering prize, the sudden fatality. We dare to imagine the former. Most of us deny the latter. Deny it, even when it confronts us.

On a chilly evening three months before he died, Tony walked into the kitchen looking stricken. Lincoln, one of his oldest childhood friends, an art professor in DC, had died of a sudden heart attack. "He was only sixty and he just dropped dead." Tony raked a hand through his hair as I hugged him. *What a crazy thing,* I thought, *to die so young and so suddenly. How awful for his wife, his kids.* I did not see how this news might relate to us. I did not think, *Tony could be Lincoln; I could be that wife.*

How could I have been so blind?

June 26, 2019

WEST TISBURY

They canceled our health insurance.

I had finally worked my way down the list of necessary chores to the task of changing our policy to cover three of us instead of four. The customer service agent put me on hold, then came back on the line to tell me my insurance had been canceled as of May 28, the day after Tony's death. Because he was the primary policyholder, the kids and I had been uninsured, in the potentially bankrupting American health care system, for a month. We would remain so until I applied for an entirely new policy, which might take weeks.

I'd already paid almost five thousand dollars to cover us that month, the rapacious sum the self-employed must fork over to adequately cover a family. That money hadn't actually bought us anything. That money, she said, would eventually be returned, but not to my account, from which it had been paid. It would be paid back to my husband's estate, which meant I wouldn't see it again till after probate.

Can this be right? Legal? Surely widows and orphans should not be thrown off their health insurance without notice, without warning. As I hung up the phone, I was shaking with anger, but also fear. What if something happened to one of us before I could get this sorted? These kids were entirely reliant on me now and yet I'd unwittingly exposed them—exposed us all—to a dangerous situation.

It's hard to explain the injustice of the United States health care system to Australians, whose taxpayer-funded Medicare covers everyone, a principle accepted by left and right alike. Australians gasp to learn how Americans are driven to bankruptcy by illness, and that lifesaving medications might cost the uninsured tens of thousands of dollars a year. I had become numb to this madness. But that someone could pay almost five grand for a month's insurance and not have any coverage was a new level of insanity.

In a crisis you understand privilege. Nathaniel had spent a college summer interning for our Massachusetts senator, Ed Markey, a champion of the Affordable Care Act. Markey's senior staff were experts in the arcana of America's messed-up health system. An email, a follow-up call, and two days later a senior executive of the insurance company was on the phone, assuring me that our coverage would be reinstated.

Once I discovered the problem, I was lucky to be able to fix it so quickly. What about all the people who didn't have a senator's office on speed dial? Who mightn't even have learned that they were uninsured until their kid had a catastrophic accident, or the pharmacy charged them hundreds—even thousands—for their lifesaving medicine?

"We are going through the wording of the Affordable Care Act," Senator Markey's staffer told me, "to see how this was even possible and what we need to do to fix it."

FLINDERS ISLAND

Even though we are moving toward the end of summer, in this deep latitude light leaves the sky at a stately pace. The horizon is still orange and the sky cobalt as I cook on a grill outside, on the deck of the shack. The shy wallabies that come by at dusk have gathered in the shadow of the tree line. I can just make out their silhouettes, curved like a calligrapher's capital *L*.

Two of my friends approach, their faces grave. How on earth did they get here?

One gently reaches out and touches my shoulder. "You said you wished there had been someone with you, the last time, so we've come here to tell you . . ."

An immense dread. I wake up, heart pounding.

The nightmare expresses my life's sudden precarity.

I absolutely cannot afford to lose anyone else.

WEST TISBURY

And finally, exactly one month after his death, the autopsy report arrived.

It was a relentless inventory of Tony's beloved body, reduced to its parts. Heart valves, kidney capsules, lung lobes, genitalia, described as "unremarkable." (Well, not to me, doctor.)

Josh and I flinched our way through it, Josh writing to say that he had been driven by the medicalized jargon to the refuge of his poetry books. He had landed on Yeats:

> *Consume my heart away; sick with desire*
> *And fastened to a dying animal*

We learned that Tony had died from "a myocarditis event" with high blood pressure and arterial disease as contributing factors.

"His heart; some long word at the heart. He is dying of a long word."
Cara, Lord Marchmain's mistress, says this to Charles Ryder in
Brideshead Revisited.

Myocarditis. Not a particularly long word. But in June 2019, I had
not heard of it. Now, post-COVID, we have all heard of myocarditis. When it showed up, especially in young men, as a rare compli-
cation of the COVID vaccine, everyone talked about it; doctors
and school nurses became alert to its symptoms.

Tony's cardiologist conferred with the medical examiner and
called me to explain the findings.

Throughout April and May, Tony's myocardium, the muscly middle
part of his heart, had been infected and inflamed. That was why he
felt short of breath when he ran for that train and played that tennis game. Late on the morning of May 27, either the inflammation,
or the scar tissue it had caused, spread to a place in the myocardium where it interrupted the delicate and complex system of elec-
trical signals that make the heart pump. The arrhythmia was fatal.

Had Tony had a virus early in the year? the doctor asked me. I
couldn't recall one. He explained that myocarditis is commonly
caused by a viral infection—an ailment that might be as trivial as a
head cold. About a third of people recover, unaware they've had it,
with only a postmortem revealing the scars it left behind. Another
third will become progressively sicker and may need all kinds of
interventions up to and including a heart transplant. The final
third, like Tony, will die suddenly. The heart, quivering instead of

pumping, fails to send blood to the brain. Without blood, without oxygen, permanent brain damage starts in four minutes, perhaps even before Mr. Ryan noticed Tony prone on Northampton Street. From that point death is only five minutes away. Tony was probably dead before the two ambulances got there.

Myocarditis typically affects young, healthy, athletic people, males twice as often as females. Although it is classified as rare, it is the third leading cause of sudden death in children and young adults.

According to the Myocarditis Foundation, symptoms—if there are any—may include shortness of breath and fatigue. "Avoiding sustained and strenuous exercise can prevent further heart damage . . . rigorous exercise and competitive sports should be avoided . . . Alcohol, particularly in excess, can increase the risk of arrhythmias and weaken an already weakened heart. Caffeinated products . . . should be avoided."

Everything Tony had been doing—even the supposedly good things like vigorous daily exercise—had been wreaking havoc on his poor sick heart.

I began to recalibrate my beliefs around his death. This was not lightning from a clear sky. He had not been a radiantly healthy man who just dropped dead. He had been sick. He had been dying, slowly, for at least two months. Dying with his arm flung over me in our bed. Dying as he wore a track in the grass, trudging to and from his study in the barn. Dying on the StairMaster at the YMCA.

From his medical records and from the emails that had passed between him and his doctor, I knew that Tony had been honest about his habits: his unhealthy alcohol consumption; his reliance on an off-label use of Provigil, a drug that powerfully boosts concentration but raises blood pressure, especially in concert with Nicorette and caffeine, which the doctor knew Tony also overused. He had counseled him on moderating his drinking; they had regular phone consultations about it, and it was helping, but not fast enough.

I should have done more. Now, I wish I'd been a nagging wife, a regular harridan, issuing ultimatums about self-destructive habits. Instead, I was the enabler, cheerfully sloshing wine into his glass at the end of the day. I hadn't taken the drinking seriously, hadn't worried about him enough. I was aware that Tony had gone to others seeking guidance, friends who'd embraced sobriety. He needed to know what their life was like on the other side of drinking; wanted reassurance that they still had fun. "When Tony called me, I was initially dismissive," one of these friends told me. "I said to him: You're a Jew; Jews aren't drunks. Then I asked him how much he drank, and, well. Whoa."

I didn't need to ask what Tony had answered. I knew.

And yet, I had convinced myself this was a short-term issue, an issue brought on by the pressures of the book, one that we could easily deal with later. And the truth is, I loved the wine-fueled fun we had together. If I'd been more conscious of the damage being done, if I'd taken better care of him and insisted on moderation, it might have bought him time—the few weeks he needed to get to those medical tests that would have disclosed his heart's perilous condition. But I can't know that; I never will know that.

What I do know: the CPR administered on the street in Chevy Chase probably never had a chance of bringing him back. Contrary to TV shows, hardly anyone who collapses with ventricular fibrillation comes back through CPR unless they are in a hospital with a code team and a crash cart. Of the 356,000 incidences of cardiac arrest outside hospitals in the United States every year, revival chances, according to *The New England Journal of Medicine*, are less than 5 percent.

Tony's cardiologist told me he was once able to interview a patient who beat these stringent odds. The man had collapsed at the dinner table and been brought back after brief CPR. "He told me he had no recollection of the event. He was just eating dinner and the next thing he knew he was on the floor, looking up at concerned faces." He reported that he had experienced no pain. No fear. No sense of an ending.

I hope that this is how it might have been for Tony, that warm morning on Northampton Street.

FLINDERS ISLAND

I haven't left Leeka since I arrived here. There is always something new to look at. The ever-changing light, the shifts in the weather, the choreography of the wallabies, the quizzical expressions of the Cape Barren geese.

But today I need to walk. I feel a sudden urge to stretch my body and do a vigorous hike. Rock-hopping north or south of here doesn't fit the bill. It's too isolated, and I must take care I don't twist an ankle on the slippery stones. I crave more heedless movement.

I apologize to the car, but we will have to brave the bumps. We navigate the road out, creaking and whining our way through fragrant forests. Ti trees are in bloom, and the eucalyptus scent is overpowering. Green rosellas swoop from branch to branch.

There is consensus in the guidebooks that there are two must-dos on the island: climb Mount Strzelecki and walk Trousers Point beach. Strzelecki is an all-day hike, and I've never loved walking straight up mountains unless I am obliged to get to the other side. I don't care about summits. There are so many good views elsewhere—why do you need to toil to a windy peak to get one? So I drive to the trailhead at Trousers Point, the beach at the western base of the mountain range.

It is indeed magnificent. Probably the loveliest beach I have ever seen; wide swoop of sand, pristine dunes, crystalline waters, a dramatic, craggy mountain backdrop. It is a juxtaposition of earth and water even more marvelous than Big Sur.

Yet I find myself unreasonably bothered by the nice barbecue facilities, the steps cut into the stone to give access to the beach, the fact that two other people show up while I am there. I've been all alone in Eden. I want to be back there.

I didn't know I would feel this way. I certainly hadn't been afraid to be by myself, but I hadn't realized how much I would embrace it. Now it is beginning to feel like an addiction. I am craving the absolute serenity of an unpeopled landscape.

And then I understand that I have not been alone. I am reveling in this time because I am with Tony. In this solitude, finally, I can think about him undistracted. I can read his journals and commune with his thoughts. I can even do what I believed his death had denied me: learn new things about him.

There are no kids, no animals, no editors, publicists, neighbors, or friends. No one, no matter how beloved, is barging in on us here. I can be beside him all my conscious day and even beyond, into my unconscious nights.

Solitude has made this space for him.

August 16, 2019

WEST TISBURY

The day finally arrived for Tony's first memorial, the one on Martha's Vineyard that I had organized. Josh would take charge of the later one in Washington, D.C. As the two events took shape, it became clear that this first gathering would center on Tony's adult life as a husband and father, writer and historian, Vineyarder. The later one would travel backward in time, focusing more on his childhood and early life, centering him as the beloved brother, uncle, student in the homeplace of his youth. As Josh and I coordinated the planning, divvying up potential speakers by who could be where in August or in October, we realized again how rich Tony's years had been: the wealth of experiences, the depth and diversity of his friendships.

I had chosen the Vineyard date at random, at a time when I was unfit to decide anything. Had I been thinking clearly, I would have realized it was the worst possible day—the absolute height of the summer season, when every airplane seat, ferry, and room on the Vineyard had been booked for months.

I had put a burden on our friends and on myself. For weeks I had been figuring out how to get friends here, how to stash them with islanders—a guesthouse here, a couch there. People had been generous offering up these spaces. In one part of my mind, I knew it would all work. The other part was in perpetual agita: Was everyone going to be okay?

A memorial is like a joyless wedding, one to which the whole world is invited, and of that infinite set of possible guests, you have only a vague idea how many will show up. The imperative to get it right—to do justice to the life—is immense. It is another thing that a grieving person is ill-equipped to do.

I had chosen a historic building that Tony loved—the Old Whaling Church in Edgartown, built by shipwrights in 1843. It is a Greek Revival structure with tall, mullioned windows that flood the interior with light. That morning, I ran around gathering flowers, arranging glasses of water for the eulogists and carpools for out-of-town guests. I put on a black dress and took my place in the front pew—the miserable seat most of us are destined to occupy someday. Bizu, handsome in a blue blazer and Tony's favorite tie, gathered his courage and walked to the podium to act as emcee, gravely welcoming and thanking those who had traveled, those who had helped.

Writers' friends are mostly writers, and the eulogies were crafted; funny, moving tributes that captured Tony's character and his accomplishments.

Martha, who got married on our Waterford porch, spoke of how hard it was to accept that Tony was no longer here. "Tony seems more here than a lot of people who actually are," she said. "Tony lit up every room he walked into. I mean, he's lighting up this one, and he's supposed to be dead."

Michael, our next-door neighbor during our years in London, made fun of Tony's compulsion for betting with friends: "He probably owes everyone in this room dinner or a bottle of wine." He observed that Tony's writing life was also a series of bets—bets he took on strangers, bets they took on him, letting him into their lives, entrusting him with their stories. "In a heavily armed world, Tony went around disarming people."

My nephew, Sam, had lived with us for a year when he was in his late twenties. He and Tony had formed a close bond, the nature of which is perhaps best summed up by the inscription Tony wrote in Sam's copy of *Confederates in the Attic*: "To Sam, a pathetic excuse for a man. With love, Tony."

I'd asked Sam to sing Bob Dylan's "Forever Young." He adjusted the microphone, strummed the first few chords, then, instead of launching into the song, he stopped and smiled wistfully. "Of course, Tony would find a way to mercilessly mock me for what's about to happen. But, here we go . . ."

Nathaniel spoke last. As a young child, he had lived in a world of imagination—a place he called his Wizarding World—where I was more comfortable joining him than Tony was. Natty's favorite books were fat fantasy novels peopled by elves and dragons, a genre I enjoyed and Tony disliked. Natty was desultory about sports, avid about his harp lessons, always writing and illustrating his own magic-filled stories, moving more in my orbit than his dad's. In his teens that began to change. He joined the high school football team, became absorbed by current events, and was an avid and capable chess player like his dad. Father and son found their interests becoming aligned. When Nathaniel was seventeen, the pair embarked on a gonzo college tour, the kind of road trip that revealed Tony at his best—connecting easily with all kinds of people, pushing open doors meant to stay closed, covering improbable distances with an itinerary always in flux if a better adventure presented itself. They returned bonded in a new, adult friendship.

We hadn't talked about what he would say in his eulogy. He walked to the podium, downed a glass of water, and took a long moment to scan the crowd. Then he spoke from the heart, without notes, without hesitation. He spoke about the consolation he took in the manner of Tony's death—that it was sudden and unforeseen. He spoke of his gratitude that each of us—he, Bizu, me—had a memory of a warm final interaction with Tony. And then he recalled that immediately after Tony's death, he found it difficult to see his father's books around the house or on the shelves at a bookstore, thinking of them as a pale shade of the father he'd lost. Then, as the weeks had passed, that changed:

"In his writing he was always at his funniest, his smartest, his most thoughtful, and his most courageous and adventurous. . . . Prose so good it would make you laugh until you cried. I recognize now that his books are not the shade of him. They're the quintessence of his soul, the distillation of a great adventurer and a good man. He's still with us through those books on our bedside tables, by the tub, in our handbags, and on our reading chairs—in our hearts, in our minds, in his words. At his best, whenever we choose to seek him out. Given the inevitability of loss, I can think of no greater consolation than that."

When our rabbi got up to say *kaddish*, I felt Josh, beside me, shaking with sobs. I could not cry. I was dried out and used up. Desiccated, gnarled.

Bizu returned to the podium to invite everyone to a reception, and as they stood to exit the pews, the razor-edged squeal of Jimi Hendrix's guitar blasted the roof off that venerable building.

"Are You Experienced?"

It was Tony's favorite song.

FLINDERS ISLAND

When I was little, I used to suffer from frequent intense fevers. My parents took me to specialists; I was always having blood drawn. They offered no firm diagnosis, and eventually I grew out of whatever it was.

When the fevers were raging, I would writhe in my parents' bed, watching the walls and ceiling bulge and recede in hallucinatory undulations. Always, at the end of it, something marvelous would happen. I would fall asleep aching and sweaty but wake up cool and free of pain, the fever suddenly gone. As the voile curtains lifted, I'd feel a breeze on my face. Through the bedroom window I'd see the red blossoms on the Christmas bush blazing against the clear blue sky. I could enjoy it again; how lovely it was. Even as a little girl, I knew to appreciate that feeling of well-being. So ordinary, until you don't have it.

I think something similar is happening to me as the days stretch out in this peaceful existence of remembered love. The days, the nights, the solitude, the dreams. I begin to feel an unfurling, an unclenching of the soul. It is a tentative thing, tender. I am afraid to probe it. If I test the idea that I might be easing into a kind of happiness, the grief might descend again, the fever still unbroken.

There's more work to do.

WEST TISBURY

In the days following the memorial, jointly and severally, the out-of-towners left the island.

Some, like Deborah, dropped in for a last visit on the way to the airport. She and her husband were the rare couple who had reported from the Mideast together as we had—she for radio, he for television. He had died just a few months earlier, a slow death from a long illness. We sat in the garden, picking at a fruit plate. She passed on some advice she received from a colleague, who had gotten it from Ruth Bader Ginsburg.

"Do your work. It might not be your best work, but it will be good work, and it will be what saves you." Deborah had followed that advice and taken her grief back into the field, reporting on the plight of Syrian refugees. I could imagine doing that: subsuming my sadness in the dire hardships of others. What I couldn't imagine was crawling back to my desk to do the work of imagination.

My mother-in-law was the last guest to leave. Ellie and I planned to have lunch at the little café at the airport before she caught her flight home to DC. As I put her bags in the trunk, she mentioned that Simba, our fluffy little rescue mutt, my mother's companion through her final years, the smallest of our dogs and yet the alpha of the household, was standing right in front of the car.

"Don't worry," I said, sliding into the driver's seat. "Simba always gets out of the way."

I pulled forward. A thud. Just this once, our seventeen-year-old dog had not moved. For a split second, I sat there, unwilling to accept what had happened. What I had just done. Then I flung myself out of the car and onto the gravel.

He was alive. He looked up at me, his huge brown eyes still trusting. I scooped up his limp body, set it on my lap, and sped right to the vet. In a panic, as I rushed to get out of the car with his soft body clutched to my heart, I forgot to put the car in park. It kept going, rolling slowly into a stand of trees. With a glance backward to see that Ellie was unharmed, I sprinted inside, yelling for the vet. It was no good. In the minutes it took to get there, Simba had died. A depression in his tiny skull disclosed that my front tire had crushed it.

In a half century of driving, I had never hit a living thing. I'd swerved around rabbits in the Outback, slammed on the brakes to avoid deer on the Vineyard. My sons chided me for pulling up short if a dead leaf fluttered across the road, just in case it was a critter. And now I'd killed my dog.

At the airport I sat with Ellie willing the minutes to pass, willing her airline to announce boarding, striving to contain my distress so as not to lay a further burden on this frail, suffering woman. Then I went home alone and dug a grave under an old cedar tree.

If 2019 had any more grief yet to come, I did not want to know of it.

FLINDERS ISLAND

This shack has two wooden daybeds on the porch, side by side, facing out to sea. On warm afternoons, I lie here with my straw hat covering my face and imagine Tony on the one next to me, engrossed in a book or catching a nap. I pretend that the silence is just the two of us sharing wordless companionship.

Night is an even better time to be out here. If the island's rocks put me in my place, its stars do, too. Nature is a remorseless reminder of human insignificance. Daytime, nighttime—there's no escape from the realization of how little we matter.

The moon has waned since I arrived on the island, and now, in the dark of a new moon, starlight alone illuminates the ocean. So many stars. The Pleiades are many more than seven sisters here, and the Milky Way streaks dense and white, luminous against the velvety black.

As a child, on summer nights, I would climb onto the corrugated iron roof of our back veranda, the metal still warm from the hot afternoon sun. I'd lie on my back and watch for shooting stars. My brain would itch, thinking of the number of galaxies whirling away into the infinite dark. Sydney is so much bigger, brighter, flashier now than it was in those days. I doubt a child in one of those inner suburbs would see much at all now. Here, the density of these visible stars reminds me of those summer nights.

"You taught me the courage of stars before you left, how light carries on endlessly, even after death." Those lyrics are from a song titled "Saturn," by Ryan O'Neal, who performs as Sleeping at Last. It is a song about a deathbed conversation, the imparting of wisdom from a dying person to a beloved survivor: that it is an extraordinary chance to have existed at all, a rare and marvelous happenstance to have lived and experienced consciousness.

Even more rare and marvelous, in this riven, aching world, to have thrived. To have found love, joy, security, fulfillment.

We had no deathbed conversation. I will never know what wisdom Tony would've wanted to impart if he'd been given the chance.

I do know this: My job is to carry his light. To keep him vibrantly illuminated for my sons, and for their children—his grandchildren—whenever they get here.

WEST TISBURY

Not long after the memorial, I drove Dizu back to school. I returned to a house empty except for the presence of our surviving dog, our lumbering, loving Bear.

I couldn't tell if it was cruel or merciful that the Vineyard September of 2019 was the most beautiful in a decade. There had been rain in the usually dry month of August, and the grass remained insistently green, even as the first leaves began to gild and blush.

I veered wildly from being thankful that this beauty was helping me get up and face the day, and bereft that Tony was not there to savor the turning leaves, the low light, the songs of the crickets and the katydids as evening drew on. Autumn was his favorite season.

Until we moved year-round to the Vineyard in 2005, September had been our summer. That was when we took our vacation, because rents on the Vineyard became less expensive, and we could find a run-down shack that we could afford to lease for a week or two. Tony had been coming to the island since he was a kid. And I, improbably, as an eleven-year-old in Sydney, had acquired a pen pal there—Joannie, whom I'd met through the Mr. Spock fan club and with whom I'd exchanged letters all through my teens and early twenties. As I've written in *Foreign Correspondence*, I'd looked forward to finally meeting her when I came to New York for grad school, but that wasn't to be: Joannie died, after a long struggle with anorexia, just months before my arrival.

Before I'd been offered the job at *The Wall Street Journal*, I had planned to head back to Sydney as soon as I had my degree. I mentioned to Tony that the Vineyard was the one place in America that I was determined to see before I went home. On Labor Day weekend in 1983, he took me there.

Tony told me later that he was relieved my pen pal hadn't hailed from an icy corner of some unlovely, blizzard-prone industrial burg. He knew I would love the natural beauty and the rural community of the Vineyard, and that the notion of a life there would be one more arrow in his quiver of arguments about the possibility of an American future.

Those stolen September weeks had been magical, especially in the years when they were our only respite from the unrelenting work of covering foreign conflicts. We'd laze on the beach, do inexpert watercolors, read poems, cook fish over driftwood fires. We'd wonder what it would be like to live on the island year-round. In 2005, when we'd both forsaken journalism for book writing, we decided to find out. We settled into life as islanders, with kids in the school and volunteer roles in the community.

But now, for all the beauty, for all the support of loving friends, I wanted to be elsewhere. I felt a desperate urge to run away from this empty home and its press of memories.

Nathaniel was living in Boston, engrossed in his job seeking out new therapies for the most intractable diseases. For winter break, Bizu had decided to go to Ethiopia, to spend December teaching English to kids at a remote rural aid compound. So after the Thanksgiving holiday, there was no need for me to stay. I found a friend to care for my dog and horse and fled to Sydney.

I arrived in the foyer of hell. The entire country was on fire; the skies dark with smoke, the news a litany of danger, delivered in unfamiliar vocabulary: ember attack, finger of fire, watch and wait, too late to leave, pyrocumulonimbus clouds, dry lightning. It was a time of anxiety, a season of lamentation.

On December 31, when the worst of the blazes had finally been brought under control, I stood with my sister in a Balmain Park overlooking Sydney Harbour and farewelled that worst of all years.

The new one, 2020, would have to be better. I believed that.

Not that I felt better. I was miserable in Sydney, because Tony and I had been so happy there.

First as newlyweds, experiencing the luxury of living together for the first time after more than a year of Midwest commutes. Later, as parents, walking Nathaniel to school. Vivid times when we were young and happy, settling into our lives as authors and realizing that against the odds this new career was going to work out for us. There were memories, everywhere. Oppressed by nostalgia, mourning the blackened bushland, the agony of burned animals, I could find no solace in Sydney.

So I ran away again, to Paris—a city in which Tony and I had no shared history. I had a writers' residency at the American Library alongside the Eiffel Tower and an apartment with old beams and a view of rooftops in the 1st arrondissement. In February the Paris grisaille matched my mood. Maybe in a new place, with new routines, I would finally be able to start writing again.

It was a half-hour walk from my apartment to the library, and every day I chose a new route, crossing the Seine on a different bridge. There was a basement office dedicated to the visiting writer, a room with no view, a departure from the bucolic outlook of trees and streams from my study at home. There would be nothing to distract me here, I thought, as I unpacked my reference books and plugged in my laptop.

That day the library director came by with a bottle of antiseptic cleaner and some wipes. "They say there is a bad virus," she said, setting them down on my desk with a shrug.

If so, no one in Paris seemed to care. The news from Italy was concerning, but Paris was in denial. Bizu arrived to spend a week of his spring break with me in Paris, before heading to lacrosse training camp in Florida. I went out to dinner with old friends from my reporting days in Kurdistan and walked home past the Louvre, stopping to admire the full moon, a disk of light poised right on the point of I. M. Pei's pyramid. I strolled by cafés and restaurants crammed with Parisiens.

Two days later, gendarmes were erecting barricades in the street outside my apartment. Restaurants didn't open. Late that night I heard Donald Trump announce he was closing America's borders. If we did not leave immediately, we might be trapped in my borrowed apartment for who knew how long, at the back of a queue in a health system I didn't know how to navigate. I threw my things into my suitcase and headed to Charles de Gaulle Airport, sitting on the floor with my laptop, booking flight after flight and then watching them get canceled. Finally, I found seats on a plane to Atlanta that was leaving in an hour. I grabbed them. It's hard to recall how little any of us knew then about what was coming. We'd scrounged for gloves and antiseptic wipes for the plane flight, but no one wore masks or knew then that they were protective.

Nathaniel was already home. He'd set up two computers in Tony's office in the barn and was working at an intense pace, the business of biotech ascendant with the need to stop this virus. Bizu's lacrosse season had been abandoned, his spring training trip canceled, his boarding school closed. I was relieved we were together, not trapped on different continents. We holed up, wondering what Tony would have made of lockdown, how his supersocial personality would have contained itself in such a narrowed world. We didn't know, then, that this pandemic would continue through the spring, into the summer, the masks and the social distancing, case spikes and anxiety lingering even into the New Year. On January 6, 2021, we watched live coverage of men with rebel flags storming the Capitol. Part of me expected to see Tony there, notebook in hand. Those white supremacists and neo-Confederates were the very people he'd sought out and interviewed, long before others paid attention, always endeavoring to understand how and why they had come to think as they did. The great American divide—North-South, urban-rural, rich-poor—had been his subject. I figured he'd probably had a beer with at least a dozen of the guys swarming those marble halls. It was a story he was made to cover, and it made me sad that he couldn't.

I was glad to have my boys at home, glad to have unexpected extra innings of mothering. Glad of the quiet. And I was glad of the end of the need to pretend that things were normal. Nothing was normal for anyone. Grief was everywhere.

Since there was to be no eating out, I threw myself into cooking. I started keeping a list of dinners, seeing how many dishes I could make before I repeated a recipe. (I made it to forty-eight.) I took long walks, befriending two calves on a neighbor's farm who came to know me, gamboling up to the stone wall when they saw me, gazing with liquid brown eyes, soliciting pats and tickles, destroying my ability to eat beef ever again.

And in this enforced, unnaturally quiet life, I edged my way back to my desk, finished the novel, and dedicated it to Tony.

FLINDERS ISLAND

As the weeks have passed, I've fallen into new habits that are particular to this place. I mark the transition between the end of the afternoon and the beginning of the evening with a long swim. The weather is usually most settled then, the wind has dropped, and the tide is highest.

Today I broke that routine and went walking late. Returning ravenous, I skip the swim. As the sun dips I regret my choice. Even though the light is fading, I walk down to the beach, throw off my clothes, and dive in.

The water is crisp on my skin but not cold. So clear that as I tread water, I can see the chips in my five-week-old pedicure. The setting sun is coloring the clouds in tones of yellow and gold.

I drop beneath the waves. It feels like a *mikveh*. I dive down, away from all the memories I've brought to the surface these past weeks.

All the noise, the pain, the nonsense of that time. I let the tug of the waves carry it all away. I come up and face this immensity of ocean.

I let the sound form, I let it uncurl like a fern. I howl, emptying my lungs.

The sound, loud and raw in this world of silence, is shocking. I let myself sink again, come up and face the blazing colors of the sky. The going down of the sun seems to mark a more final ending than simply a day. This day, any day, could be the last day. We all know that. Now I feel it.

I take the weight of it and hurl it back into the air, another howl. Under again, then toward the east, the place of the first light. The light Tony will never see again. I wail for him, for the life he no longer has, for the life we no longer have together.

When I turn back toward the shack, there's nothing left. I am spent, at last. All that remains is a long exhalation, a sustained sigh.

When I started to write fiction, I came across a piece of advice on the craft of novel writing. Your task, as novelist, is to keep pushing your protagonist's head under water throughout the narrative. But when you get to the end, you must decide: Will you sink them, or let them swim?

I put my face in the clear, briny water. I stretch out my body.

I swim.

AFTERWORD

Nice ending, *nu?*

But it's not the end. Not the end of grieving for Tony. That will go on.

It will get worse at times, I know it. When Nathaniel is a bridegroom, when Bizu graduates from college, when one of them becomes a father. They will likely marry people who never knew Tony, who will have no memories of him to pass on to his grandchildren. I will grieve this. And I will grieve the grandfather that Tony would have been: the funny *zaydeh* who encouraged his grandkids to do crazy things. The *zaydeh* whose grandkids adored him.

So, not the end of grieving. Not even the end of my stay in the shack. I had more days there. I swam, I wrote, I read Tony's journals, I visited the Mother Rock and offered whatever comes closest to prayer for someone without a recipient address. I found a place on the shore that looked like a carefully planted rock garden. There among the heaved-up boulders and the scouring salt, bright purple blooms of ice plant and cool green euphorbias filled the crevices. Life, exerting itself.

I embraced the solitude, accompanied only by wallabies, pademelons, even, at last, a lone, waddling wombat. I hoarded the quiet, before the return to the noisy world.

Yes, if I hadn't met Tony, I believe I could have had a good life on Flinders Island: a wind-burned, flannel-clad writer and gardener, volunteering at the tiny school and with environmental groups, crankily opposing inappropriate development. There is no way to see who would have stood beside me in that alternative life, what kids we might or might not have had together. So I let those speculations go, cast into the blustery winds. I resolve to appreciate the life I have had, surrounded by love, in another rare and beautiful place.

I have written this because I needed to do it. Part of the treatment for "complicated grief" is to relive the trauma of the death, returning to the moments again and again, striving each time to recall more detail. That's what I have tried to do.

"The predicament when writing about a sudden, untimely death: the more you remember, the more elusive that death becomes," writes the novelist Yiyun Li. I have not found that to be true. I have brought Tony's death with me to the place where I could relive it, slowing it down and taking it in, suffering it in the way I needed to suffer.

There are memories that remain elusive, moments that resist recall. I can't remember the words I used to tell Bizu that his dad had died. The blackness that descended as I listened to his sobs has expunged that memory. My first conversation with Nathaniel also is a blur. All I remember of it is the shock of realizing that he already knew—that someone else's words had flown around the world to him faster than my own.

The day after I got home from Washington, D.C., a dear friend, a widower, was one of the first people who insisted on coming to see me. He had advice for me, he said, that could not wait: the three most salient lessons of his own loss. Make it safe for people to talk about Tony, he said. The first time he had ventured out after losing his beloved wife, Gretchen, no one had mentioned her, and he had been hurt and angered. He realized that he needed to speak of her first, to allow others to do so. This was excellent advice, and I still follow it, bringing Tony with me into every conversation.

Don't come home to a silent house, he said. Leave the radio on. Since I had two dogs at the time, both enthusiastic greeters, I told him I didn't expect that would be a problem for me.

But what was the third thing he said?

I know it was good advice; I know I followed it. Whatever it was, it is gone now—buried in my chaotic memories of those first days. Lost as surely as the third decimal place for pi and the capital city of Benin.

Now, back in the press of people, the loud routines of my real, often public life, I can begin to assess how this self-administered therapy has worked. One thing was apparent right away: my time alone in nature restored me, as nature always does. In the novel *Tom Lake*, Ann Patchett's protagonist observes: "I know the suffering exists beside wet grass and a bright blue sky recently scrubbed by rain. The beauty and the suffering are equally true."

At home now I make more time for the beauty. I make it a point to notice the trees, in all their various seasonal personalities. To be with the critters that share my space. A nest of baby rabbits, a coin-sized painted turtle hatchling, a fluffy mallard duckling out for its first swim—these encounters, more than almost anything else, have the power to elevate me out of sadness.

And another thing I have noticed. The time on Flinders Island allowed me to set down one of the bundles in the baggage of my grief. It's the grief I had been carrying for the life I would have had, the life I had counted on having. It was the life with the sunset-facing rocking chairs, growing old with Tony beside me, laughing, arguing over the news, revisiting shared memories, and taking pride as our sons moved confidently into manhood. That life is gone; nothing will get it back. I have accepted that. I have embarked on making the life I have as vivid and consequential as I can. Do your work, said Bader Ginsburg. So, that is what I do.

I have written here with a faint and modest agenda. There are things that I wish could be different. I'm not sure if our modern secular world has the capacity to come up with a gentler way of dealing with bereavement. I don't know if we can make room for something like Sorry Business, *iddah*, *sheloshim*, *chehelom*.

I merely wish for the bereaved some time and space, however long, however short, for melancholy—what Victor Hugo described as the happiness of being sad.

Our culture is averse to sad. We want people to be happy. We're chagrined and slightly offended when they're not. There is a desire to cheer them up. And then, later, there will be a glancing at the wristwatch, a tapping of the foot if they cannot be cheered, if their grief is perceived to go on too long. I wish we could resist those things.

I also hope that the medical-forensic establishment in the United States might reevaluate its inhumane practices, develop better protocols for how to break this worst of news, how to handle beloved bodies and their mourners in the immediate hours after death.

In her book *Any Ordinary Day*, the journalist Leigh Sales looks at what happens to people when their world is suddenly upended by trauma and loss. The cases she documents are all well-known Australian tragedies. In all of them police, and sometimes clergy, arrive in person to break the news to the next of kin. No one calls and blurts it out over the phone. One case Sales describes is that of Matt Richell, a young publisher fatally injured when thrust into rocks in a surfing accident. When his wife, Hannah, went to the morgue to view his body, she was met by a woman who described in detail what she would encounter: the layout of the room she would enter, what he was wearing, the color of the sheet that covered him, what the wounds on his face and head would look like. She told Hannah she could go in alone or accompanied, and that she could stay as long as she liked.

It is a strange thing to say you envy someone their visit to a morgue, but as I read that account, I envied Hannah. How hard could it be, really, to afford the bereaved this small measure of humanity? A modicum of empathy. It's not a lot to ask.

Yet institutional practices are hard to change. So, I have a proposal that is an individual practice, something anyone can do—a simple habit for people in a long partnership. Jot down all the tasks you don't bother to mention that keep the household afloat, the set of torches that only you have learned to juggle. All the little things your partner didn't expect to need to know, until the day they never expected to happen.

If it had been me who died suddenly, I am entirely sure that Tony wouldn't have known where to find the stop valve for the water if a pipe burst, or even the name of the plumber to call to fix it. He probably would've struggled to find the kids' vaccination records or the URL and password to access their report cards. Those were in my task basket, just as so many other things were in his. I suggest that everyone make a document. Call it *Your Life: How It Works* and periodically update it. If I'd had such a document, it would have freed me from time-consuming material tasks and allowed more space to do the necessary work of grieving.

And finally, in whatever way works for you, tell your story.

Write it down, speak it to a therapist, share it with your friends. Take control of this essential moment in the narrative of your life. When he was still in hiding after Ayatollah Khomeini's fatwa, Salman Rushdie surfaced to make a speech at Columbia University. "Those who do not have power over the story that dominates their lives, the power to retell it, rethink it, deconstruct it, joke about it, and change it as times change, truly are powerless," he said.

This story of a death is the story that dominates my life. Here I have retold it, rethought it. But I can't change it. Tony is dead. Present tense. He will be dead, in the present, in my present, for as long as I am alive. I cannot change that story. I can only change myself.

Write the truest thing you know, said old man Hemingway.

Dear reader, this is it.